Computer Programming

A Practical Course in
FORTRAN IV

C. Tomasso, B.Sc.

LONDON
W. FOULSHAM & CO. LTD.
NEW YORK · TORONTO · CAPETOWN · SYDNEY

W. FOULSHAM & CO. LTD.,
Yeovil Road, Slough, Bucks., England

ISBN 0-572-00766-3
© C. Tomasso 1971

PRINTED BY PHOTO-LITHOGRAPHY AND MADE IN GREAT BRITAIN
AT THE PITMAN PRESS, BATH

Computer Programming

A Practical Course in FORTRAN IV

Preface

This text is prepared by the Teacher-in-Charge of the Glasgow Schools' Computer Centre 1 (Dundas Vale). It is intended to cover a basic course in Fortran IV Computer Studies for pupils following an academic certificate course in the Sciences. The course of study is so arranged that pupils make contact with the computer shortly after the initialising assignments. It covers sufficient ground to enable pupils to apply computer methods to a variety of subjects within their school syllabus or commercial fields.

The content of this course will appeal to pupils and teachers alike, for the author is a practising teacher with experience in teaching Mathematics and Science at all levels in the secondary school and with experience in the computer industry.

This book is the outcome of an experimental set of assignments tried out in the classroom and modified in the light of experience. The approach to the content is exciting and the presentation modern—the pupil is encouraged to study individually at his own pace and to apply his knowledge of computer methods to 'problem solving' over a varied field.

The text appears at a most appropriate period in time—teachers are seeking tried classroom material for computer studies, a recent addition to the syllabus. With the raising of the school-leaving age, such material will be in demand. Teachers will find this particular material most helpful, not least in the stimulus it will provide to fresh and purposeful thinking on their own part—that I am certain should be an essential feature of any worthwhile textbook.

Apart from its obvious school application, the material provides useful and stimulating practical sessions for business computer courses and commercial studies outside the classroom environment.

This text presents a challenge to pupils and makes valuable contribution to the library in this field.

I. D. WATT

ADVISER IN MATHEMATICS, CORPORATION
OF GLASGOW EDUCATION DEPARTMENT

Foreword

This set of Practical Sessions is intended as an introduction to the computer language of Fortran. The Practical Sessions are presented in such a way that the student experiences the minimum of delay before writing a program which will run successfully on a computer. By gradually increasing the instruction repertoire the assignments build up to a point where the natural extension is to a study of function and sub-routine usage.

The assignments were originally intended for pupils in their fourth year at secondary school. But it was soon found that they were also suitable for fifth- and sixth-year pupils as a quick introduction to Fortran. At third-year level, too, although the pace was slower, the assignments were also found to be useful, provided that suitable supplementary problems for programming could be given.

Many of the questions given in the exercises, especially in the initial stages, are closely related to the worked examples. This is done to give the pupil confidence in the crucial early stages of program writing. The advantage of an assignment technique based on graded worked examples and exercises is that it allows a pupil to proceed at his own pace. Also, it allows the teacher more time to concentrate on pupils who might experience real difficulty.

The assignments have been used with much success in Glasgow Secondary Schools' Computer Centre No. 1. Pupils attend the Centre once a week for two and a half hours. Half of this time is devoted to a practical, 'hands-on' session using the computer as a tool in problem solving. The rate of program writing varies from two programs a week in the second and third years to four programs a week in the fifth and sixth years. The assignments have also proved to be useful in the classroom if some means of having the programs run on a computer exist.

C. Tomasso

Contents

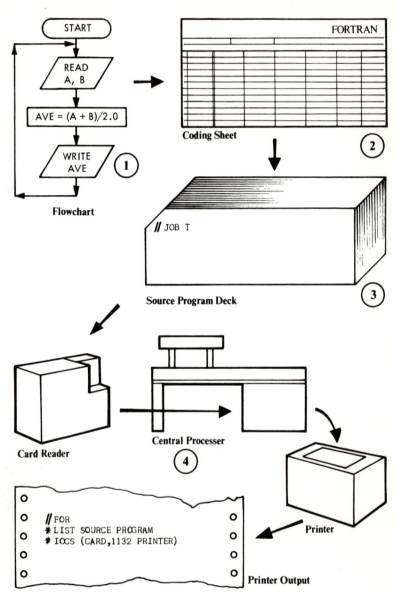

START

READ
A, B

AVE = (A + B)/2.0

WRITE
AVE ①

Flowchart

FORTRAN

Coding Sheet ②

// JOB T

Source Program Deck ③

Card Reader

Central Processer ④

Printer

// FOR
* LIST SOURCE PROGRAM
* IOCS (CARD,1132 PRINTER)

Printer Output

Stages in problem solving by computer

Introduction

Much has been written about computers and how they work. It is the intention of this set of Practical Sessions to concentrate on how the computer is used as a tool in solving mathematical problems.

Program Preparation

In preparing any problem for solution by computer the sequence of actions is as follows:

Stage 1: Prepare a flowchart
Stage 2: Write a Fortran program on a coding sheet.
Stage 3: Transfer the instructions on the coding sheet onto punched cards.
Stage 4: Load and run the program on the computer.

In the diagram opposite 1, 2 and 3 depict the three stages involved in program preparation, while 4 depicts the automatic execution of the program which produces the final printed answers. Let us now consider each stage in turn.

Stage 1

In solving any problem on the computer we must first make out a plan of attack. This is the job of the *flowchart*, which is a diagram outlining the various steps the computer must take to produce the required solution of the problem.

The most common symbols used in flowchart construction are these:

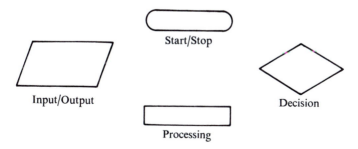

Start/Stop

Input/Output

Processing

Decision

By making use of these symbols, we can prepare a flowchart, say, to find the average of two numbers A and B:

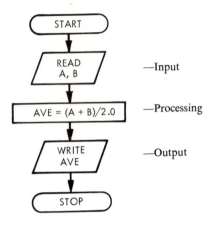

In the Practical Sessions which follow flowcharts will be used to clarify the method adopted in solving the various worked examples.

Stage 2

A special form, called a Fortran coding form, is used to code the instructions outlined by the flowchart into Fortran. An example of a completed coding form for the problem in question is shown opposite. For completeness the form includes the necessary control cards that are required by every program as well as the Fortran instructions. Control cards differ from one kind of machine to another. But the coded Fortran instructions do not vary greatly between one machine and another. All programs in these Practical Sessions are written specifically for IBM 1130 computers. Little in the way of change, apart from using different control cards, need be done to run these programs on other computers.

The coding form contains 80 columns. The 80 columns on the coding sheet bear a one-to-one correspondence with the 80 columns on the punched card. Thus, each line of information on the coding sheet represents the information to be punched onto each card and in precisely the same column as it appears on the coding sheet.

Fortran Coding Form

GLASGOW SECONDARY SCHOOLS COMPUTER CENTRE 1

Programmer	A. NAME		Problem	
Date 1Ø/JAN/71	Page 1 of 1		TO FIND THE AVERAGE OF TWO NUMBERS	

```
STATE-    LABEL 73 76
MENT
1 No.5 6 7        10        20        30        40        50        60        70   SERIAL 77 80
// JOB T
// FOR
*LIST SOURCE PROGRAM
*IOCS(CARD,1132 PRINTER)
C      TO FIND THE AVERAGE OF TWO REAL NUMBERS
       READ(2,1Ø)A,B
1Ø     FORMAT(2F1Ø.3)
       AVE=(A+B)/2.Ø
       WRITE(3,2Ø)AVE
2Ø     FORMAT(15X,F1Ø.3)
       CALL EXIT
       END
// XEQ
       21.6ØØ    315.584
```

Completed coding form for program to find the average of two numbers A and B

11

Line 7 of the coding sheet on page 11 would appear on a punched card as follows:

```
10 FORMAT(2F10.3)
  ▌  ▌▌▌ ▌
     ▌▌▌        ▌
0000▌0C0C00▌CC00▌C000000000C0000000000000030C0000C000000000000000000CC000C0000C00000000
1234567891011121314151617181920212223242526272829303132333435363738394041424344454647484950515253545556575859606162636465666768697071727374757677787980
111▌11111▌1▌111▌1111111111111111111111 .11111111111111111111111111111111111111111111!!1
222222222222▌222222222222:222222222222:22222222222222222222222222222222222222222:2222222
33333333333▌33333▌▌33333333333333333333333333333333333333333333333333333333333333333
444444444▌4444444444444444444444444444444444444444444444444444444444444444444444444444
55555555555▌555555▌5555555555555555555555555555555555555555555555555555555555555555555
66666▌▌666666▌666666666666666666666666666666666666666666666666666666666666666666666666
7777777777777777777777777777777777777777777777777777777777777777777777777777777777777
888888888888▌8888▌8▌88898888888888888888888888888888888888888888888888888888888888888
9999999▌999999999999999999999999999999999999999999999999999999999959999999999999999999
1234567891011121314151617181920212223242526272829303132333435363738394041424344454647484950515253545556575859606162636465666768697071727374757677787980
M°CORQUODALE.I
```

Punched card for line 7 of the coding sheet on page 11

It is essential that information, whether instructions or data, is correctly punched onto cards. Since there is always some confusion between certain alphabetic and numeric characters, the following convention has been adopted when filling in the coding sheet:

Ø indicates a zero, whereas an O indicates an alphabetic O
1 ,, ,, one, ,, ,, I ,, ,, ,, I
2 ,, ,, two, ,, ,, Z ,, ,, ,, Z

The coding sheet is divided into various sections by a series of heavy vertical lines. This is because the various groups of columns formed by these lines are used for different purposes, a list of which is given below.

Column allocation

Note	Column	Purpose
(1)	1	Used to punch a C for comments cards.
(2)	2–5	Used for statement numbers.
(3)	6	Punched to indicate a continuation card.
(4)	7–72	Used for Fortran statements.
(5)	73–80	Not used by Fortran. Can be used for identification.

Note

(1) If a C is punched in card column 1 then any comment placed in columns 2 to 80 inclusive will be printed in the Source Listing (described in Stage 4). Any number of comment cards may be used.

12

(2) All Fortran statements which require referencing are allocated a number. Statement numbers can lie in the range 1 to 9999, but under no circumstances may two statements have the same number. Any Fortran statement may be given a statement number, but only those statements referred to elsewhere in the program need have any. There is no need to have these numbers in sequence, although it is more usual to do so. There are no commas placed between the thousands and the hundreds.

(3) Any character other than a zero or a blank may be punched in column 6 when a Fortran statement that was too long for the previous card is continued on the current card. If there is more than one continuation card involved in a Fortran statement, then it is common practice to use a 1 for the first continuation card, a 2 for the second, a 3 for the third, and so on.

(4) Any legal Fortran statement may be placed in these columns, which is syntactically correct according to the rules of the language.

(5) These final columns are always ignored by Fortran. They can, for example, be punched with a sequential set of numbers. Then, if the cards become disarranged, they can quickly be put back in order.

Stage 3

When the coding sheet is complete, each line (each Fortran statement) is transferred to a punched card, and the resultant card deck is called the *source program deck*. Here is an example:

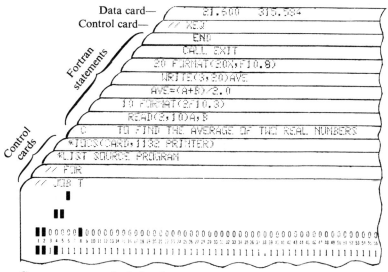

Source program deck for the program on page 11

Stage 4

The source program deck is fed into the computer, which has a resident program capable of converting the Fortran program into electrical impulses, or patterns of ones and zeros that the machine can understand. These ones and zeros are machine instructions called *machine language*. The resident program is called the Fortran compiler. There are many compilers available on the computer, each for a different computer language, such as ALGOL, COBOL and TAM. As well as translating, the compiler checks to make sure that there are no syntactical mistakes, such as missing commas or brackets or malformed instructions. If the program is found to be error free, it will be executed. If not, an error message will be printed to indicate not only the type of error but its whereabouts in the program. Shown below is the source listing and printed result (last line) of the program described earlier.

```
PAGE    1

// JOB T

LOG DRIVE    CART SPEC    CART AVAIL    PHY DRIVE
   0000         0002         0002          0000

V2 M07    ACTUAL  8K  CONFIG  8K

// FOR
*LIST SOURCE PROGRAM
*IOCS(CARD,1132 PRINTER)
C         TO FIND THE AVERAGE OF TWO REAL NUMBERS
          READ(2,10)A,B
      10 FORMAT(2F10.3)
          AVE=(A+B)/2.0
          WRITE(3,20)AVE
      20 FORMAT(20X,F10.3)
          CALL EXIT
          END

FEATURES SUPPORTED
  IOCS

CORE REQUIREMENTS FOR
  COMMON      0  VARIABLES      6  PROGRAM      58

  END OF COMPILATION

// XEQ

              168.592
```

Summary of the Control Cards Required

All programs throughout these Practical Sessions will contain the necessary control cards for operation on the IBM 1130 computing system. A summary of the cards used and their sequence of appearance in all programs is shown opposite.

14

Fortran Coding Form

GLASGOW SECONDARY SCHOOLS COMPUTER CENTRE 1

Programmer	A. NAME		Problem	
Date 1∅/JAN/71	Page 1 of 1		CONTROL CARDS SUMMARY FOR IBM 1130 SYSTEM	LABEL 73 76

STATE-MENT 1 2 No. 5 6 7	10	20	30	40	50	60	70	SERIAL 77 80
// JOB T								
// FOR								
*LIST SOURCE PROGRAM								
*IOCS(CARD,1132 PRINTER)								
			{ FORTRAN PROGRAM STATEMENTS					
// XEQ			{ DATA (if any)					

Summary of control cards for IBM 1130 computing system

15

Practical Session 1
Types of Number

Real and Integer Numbers

The numbers with which computers deal are either (i) integer numbers, or (ii) real numbers.

Examples of *integer numbers* are:

        6   264   10   11629   1056

The above numbers have two distinct features:

(*a*) They have no decimal point. It is assumed that the point is always positioned at the extreme right-hand side of the number but is never actually written. For this reason, integer numbers are sometimes known as *fixed-point* numbers.

(*b*) They have no comma separating the thousands from the hundreds.

(*Note:* No integer number on IBM 1130 may be greater than 32767 or less than −32768.)

Examples of *real numbers* are

  1·2   65·4   101·45   ·12 1·   0·   ·0005   16543·8

The notable features of the above numbers are:

(*a*) They each contain a decimal point.

(*b*) Once again they have no comma separating the thousands from the hundreds.

(*Note*: No real number on IBM 1130 may be greater than 10^{38} or less than 10^{-39}.)

Numbers, whether integer or real, can be stored in the computer's memory. This is done by choosing a convenient name for the quantity in question and then assigning the numerical value of this quantity to the named memory location. For example, a man might earn £21·5 per week. A convenient name for this quantity could be PAY. The numerical value of 21·5 could then be assigned or stored in the named memory location called PAY by an appropriate instruction. Each time PAY is mentioned in the program the computer uses the value 21·5. At any stage in the program, by using a suitable instruction, the contents of PAY can be changed to some other value. Because the contents of named locations in memory may be changed, if desired, in the course of a program, these names are called *variables*.

To deal with the two number types, integers and real numbers, two types of variables exist. They are integer variables (integer names) and real variables (real names). The rules governing these different name types are given below.

Rules for naming variables

(1) *All* variable names must consist of no more than *five* alphabetic and/or numeric characters. No special characters such as (, +, −, . , ? and so on, are allowed.

(2) *All* variable names must begin with an alphabetic character.

(3) *Real* variables must begin with one of these letters:

A, B, C, D, E, F, G, H, O, P, Q, R, S, T, U, V, X, Y, Z

(4) *Integer* variables must begin with one of these letters:

I, J, K, L, M, N

Thus you can recognise whether a variable is real or integer from the first letter of the variable name. If you remember the set of letters for integer naming, that is, *I* to *N* inclusive, there is no need to remember the set of letters for real naming, since they consist of the remaining letters of the alphabet. The word *IN*teger is an aid to remembering this.

Examples of valid and invalid integer variables

Valid	Invalid	Reason
I	4I	First character must be alphabetic.
IT	J+K	No special characters allowed.
JAM	AMT	Integer variable names do not begin with an *A*.
M123	INTEREST	Too long.

Examples of valid and invalid real variables

Valid	Invalid	Reason
X	AMOUNT	Too long.
HOURS	HRS,	No special characters allowed.
PAY	MONEY	Real variables do not begin with an *M*.
D627	6PAY	Must not begin with a numeric.
ABLE1	ABLE 1	No blanks allowed.

Arithmetic Statements

Special use of the 'equals' sign

Earlier it was stated that there was an appropriate instruction for assigning numerical values to named variables. In fact there are two such instructions commonly used. The first is the READ instruction, but this will be dealt with in Practical Session 2. The second is the arithmetic instruction which we shall study now.

The 'equals' sign, as used in Fortran, is always interpreted as an assignment symbol. In its simplest form an assignment statement or arithmetic statement which places the value 21·5 into the variable PAY is:

$$PAY = 21.5$$

Similarly, the variable GROSS may be assigned the same value as that contained in PAY by using the expression:

$$GROSS = PAY$$

It is important to note that had GROSS contained, say, the value 10·4, this value would be replaced by 21·5 if the above instruction were performed.

The simple rule illustrated above always applies with Fortran, that is, the numerical quantity stated or represented by the expression on the right-hand side of the 'equals' sign is always assigned to the variable situated on the left-hand side.

Arithmetic Expressions

By making use of the symbols for addition, subtraction, multiplication, division and exponentiation listed below, arithmetic expressions can be made as complex as required.

Symbol	Operation
+	Addition
−	Subtraction
*	Multiplication
/	Division
**	Exponentiation

(*Note*: The double symbol ** means 'raise to the power of',
     e.g. x^3 would be written x**3 i.e. x raised to the power of 3.)

Because Fortran is designed specifically to handle algebraic formulae, **it is not** surprising to find that many of the normal rules for expression evaluation apply. The order in which an expression is evaluated is given below:

(a) First priority—brackets
(b) Second priority—exponentiation
(c) Third priority— multiplication and division
(d) Fourth priority—addition and subtraction

Where operations of the same priority occur together, they are evaluated from left to right, i.e.

$$X = A/B*C$$

$$\text{means } x = \frac{ac}{b} \text{ not } \frac{a}{bc}$$

The following examples illustrate the use both of the operations and the priority rules.

Original mathematical statement	Equivalent Fortran statement	
$a = c^3$	A = C**3	
$s = t^2 - r$	S = T**2 - R	
$x = \left(\dfrac{a+b}{a-b}\right)^2 - d$	X = ((A + B)/(A - B))**2 - D	
$u = \dfrac{v}{(v-3\cdot0)^3}$	U = V/(V - 3.0)**3	
$y = \dfrac{c}{d} - \dfrac{ef}{gh}$	Y = C/D - (E*F)/(G*H) Y = C/D - E/G*F/H	or
$r = \dfrac{(s)^{n-1}}{t}$	R = S**(N - 1)/T	
$x = (y^r)^t$	X = (Y**R)**T	
$z = a(2b + c)$	Z = A*(2.0*B + C)	

Exceptions to the normal rules of algebra

(1) Only one variable may appear on the left-hand side of the '=' sign:

X - A = B**2	unacceptable
X = B**2 + A	acceptable

(2) If multiplication is intended, then it must be specifically stated, i.e. no implied multiplication is allowed:

ANS = 2.5(A + B)	unacceptable
ANS = 2.5*(A + B)	acceptable

(3) Two operators may not appear side by side:

PROD = A* — B	unacceptable
PROD = A*(—B)	acceptable

Counting

The special use of the 'equals' symbol leads to what appears to be an absurd mathematical statement:

$$KOUNT = KOUNT + 1$$

How can any number be equal to one greater than itself? Of course, this is not what is meant by the statement. Since the '=' symbol is used as an assignment symbol in Fortran, the statement really means that 1 has to be added to the current value of the variable KOUNT and that this result is to be assigned back to the variable KOUNT. Thus, after execution of this arithmetic statement, KOUNT has a value one greater than it had before execution.

If this statement were now to be repeated over and over again, the corresponding values assigned to KOUNT would increase by one each time. This type of arithmetic statement in Fortran is very useful, as will be demonstrated in Practical Session 3.

The same variable KOUNT can be increased by amounts other than 1, e.g.

$$KOUNT = KOUNT + 10$$

This would lead, on repetition of the above statement, to the value of KOUNT being increased by the amount 10 each time.

Totals can also be accumulated by this technique. If, say, the variable TOTAL is used to store the total pay, the appropriate arithmetic instruction is:

$$TOTAL = TOTAL + PAY$$

If PAY can have different assigned values each time the above statement is executed, then the sum total of all the PAYs can be accumulated by the variable TOTAL.

Mode of an Expression

Because the computer handles real numbers in an entirely different fashion from integer numbers, it is usual to keep all variables and constants in any single expression in the same *mode*. Only the variables and constants of the right-hand side of the expression need be considered to determine the mode. Powers are not taken into consideration.

Here is how to determine the mode:

(a) If all variables and constants on the right-hand side of an expression (excluding powers) are real variables and constants, the expression is said to be in *real mode*.

(*b*) If all variables and constants on the right-hand side of an expression (excluding powers) are integer variables and constants, the expression is said to be in *integer mode*.

Consider the following examples:

Expression	Mode
ANS = 2.0*(A/B - C)	Real
IANS = 2.0*(A/B - C)	Real
B = A**2	Real
X = I**2	Integer
Y = 2*(I - J/K)	Integer

Integer division

Integer division causes some surprising results, as you can see below:

I = 2/3	then I = 0
A = 2/3	then A = 0.0
K = 4/3	then K = 1
A = 4/3	then A = 1.0
N = 9/2	then N = 4

If division is carried out in integer mode, truncation of any decimal fraction takes place. This has its advantages for programming purposes as will be seen later. Care must be exercised in using integer mode expressions. If the variable on the left-hand side is a real variable, truncation still takes place, but when the result is assigned to the real variable, the truncated result is made real.

Assignment 1

(1) Which of the following numbers are integer and which are real?

(i) 1·0	(ii) 64·5	(iii) 112
(iv) 1·	(v) 13	(vi) 17441·0
(vii) 1	(viii) 16·4	(ix) 0

(2) What is the predominant type of number in the list of numbers given below, and which number or numbers do not belong to this type?

14   62·4   916·0   916·   916   2645·1

(3) Below is given a set of integer and real numbers, some of which have a fault in common. What is the fault?

2,164·1   6129   3,456   21544·1   15,642

(4) Tick those examples which you think are correct variable names.

Integer variables	Real variables
ITEMS	SUM
D/DAY	G.B.
MO	X
3INT	TOTL
JJJJ	W54321
N6785	(ABLE)
ALAN	DON'T

(5) Indicate whether the following statements are true or false by placing a *T* after those which are true and an *F* after those which are false.
  (i) A real variable name is always six characters long.
  (ii) An integer variable name is always five characters long.
  (iii) Integer variable names can begin with a special character, whereas real variables must not.
  (iv) It is permissible to combine numeric characters with alphabetic characters when constructing variable names.
  (v) There are three types of variable names.

(6) Opposite each of the following items of data give a suitable variable name to accommodate that data.

Numerical data	Variable name
2	....
2·14567	....
2·	....
·1	....
0	....
2654	....

(7) State what is wrong with each of the following expressions:
  (i) X = 2.5A
  (ii) Y = (A − B/2.0)*3.5)
  (iii) X1 = (−B ± DISCM)/2.0A
  (iv) SELLP − COSTP = PROFIT
  (v) T = A***3

(8) Convert to normal mathematical notation the following Fortran expressions:

e.g. X = A**2 - B**2   is $x = a^2 - b^2$

(i) A = 2*0/X - 4.5

(ii) S = A/B*C

(iii) B = (A**2)**3

(iv) Y = ((S**2 - T)/R)**(N - 1)

(9) Convert the following mathematical expressions into equivalent Fortran statements:

e.g. $x = \dfrac{a}{bc}$ is   X = A/B/C   or   X = A/(B*C)

(i) $y = \dfrac{2 \cdot 5a}{c}$

(ii) $s = \dfrac{(r - t)^2}{t}$

(iii) $a = \dfrac{xy}{4} - \dfrac{stu}{x}$

(iv) $h = r^{n-1}$

(v) $c = \left\{\dfrac{(a - b)}{(a - d)}\right\}^{n-1}$

(10) If the variables A, B and C are assigned the values 2·0, 6·0 and 3·5, state the value assigned to X in each of the following:

(i) X = A**2 - B

(ii) X = 10.0*(C - A/B)

(iii) X = (A - B)**2

(iv) X = (A**2)**3

(11) Perform the following instructions in the sequence stated and give the value of X:

(i) S = 4.5
    T = 6.0
    R = 3.0
    X = (S - R)**2 - T

(ii) X = 5.0
    Y = 3.0
    Z = X - Y
    X = (Z**2)/2.0 + Z/(X - 1.0)*Y

(12) State the mode of the following expressions.

(i) Y = 2.5/A - B*C

(ii) Z = I/J

(iii) I = A/B*C - D

(iv) ANS = A**3

(v) MONSL = ANSAL/12.0 - TAX

(13) Find the value of *S* by performing the various operations in sequence.

(i) T = 2/3
    R = T + 10.5
    S = R/2.0

(ii) A = 6.0
    I = A/4.0
    S = I + 2*I

(14) State which of the expressions below is of mixed mode.

(i) Y = A**3 − 2

(ii) A = I/J − 2*N

(15) It is required to store the answer of the arithmetic statement with at least two decimal places. Which of these two statements should be used?

(i) IPAY = HOURS*RATE

(ii) PAY = HOURS*RATE

Practical Session 2
Input and Output

Consider a program to read the values of the variables A and B, add them and then print out the answer. Even with such a trivial task as this, there are two immediate difficulties:

(a) The reading of the values of A and B into the computer, that is, *input*.

(b) The writing out of the answer by the computer, that is, *output*.

Input

Consider a data card containing the two real numbers 21·600 and 315·584:

1	2	3	4	5	6	7	8	9	10	11	12	13	14	15	16	17	18	19	20	21	22	23	24	25	26
			2	1	.	6	0	0					3	1	5	.	5	8	4						

The two numbers can be assigned to the variables A and B respectively by reading them from the data card. A pair of Fortran statements which would accomplish this are:

```
          READ (2,10) A, B
       10 FORMAT (2F10.3)
```

When data is to be read from cards, two statements are always required (i) a READ statement and (ii) a FORMAT statement.

The READ statement

(1) The elements of the statement are as follows:

READ is always used at the beginning of every input statement.

2   is the unit number of the card reader. Since reading on a computer can be accomplished by any one of many input devices, each is allocated a unit number to avoid confusion.

10   is the arbitrary number chosen for the accompanying FORMAT statement.

A is the first variable to which data read from the data card is assigned.

25

> *B* is the second variable to which data read from the data card is assigned.

(2) The brackets and commas in the READ statement are important.

(3) The list of variables which appears after the brackets can contain as many variables as are required. They must be separated from each other by commas.

Generalising, all READ statements must be written as specified below:

> READ (Unit no., Format no.) List of variables
> separated by commas

The FORMAT statement

Consider a data card containing the two real numbers 21·600 and 315·584:

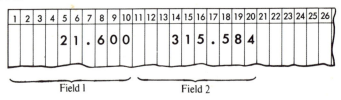

The two values 21·600 and 315·584, which are to be stored by *A* and *B* respectively, can be positioned anywhere on the data card. The first number occupies the first 10 card columns and the second number occupies the second 10 card columns. The data card has thus been divided into two segments which are called *fields*. The first field and the second field both have a width of 10 card columns. They need not necessarily have the same field widths, although they usually do.

Each real number occupying a field is coded separately according to the formula:

$$Fw.d$$

where *F*—is the code for a real number,

    w—is the field width,

    . —is always required,

    d—is the number of decimal digits occupying the field. If there are no decimal digits, *d* should be specified by a 0.

Hence the number in field 1 is coded F10.3 and similarly the number in field 2 is coded F10.3.

The FORMAT statement describing the above data card can therefore be written as:

    10 FORMAT (F10.3, F10.3)

or more concisely   10 FORMAT (2F10.3)

In general terms every FORMAT statement can be summed up by the expression:

> n FORMAT (Field specifications, separated by commas if more than one specification)

Note

(1) n is the necessary statement number of the FORMAT statement and is always referenced by a READ statement or a WRITE statement.

(2) The brackets enclosing the field specifications are necessary.

Example 1

(In this example two of the input values have the same field width, while the third value has a different field width.) Read in three numbers from the data card shown and assign these values to the variables AMPS, VOLTS and Q respectively.

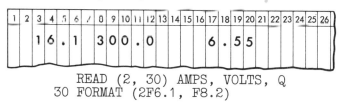

```
        READ (2, 30) AMPS, VOLTS, Q
     30 FORMAT (2F6.1, F8.2)
```

Note

(1) The format number in the READ statement agrees with the number of the FORMAT statement.

(2) The value 16·1 is assigned to AMPS
                300·0   ,,   ,,   ,, VOLTS
        and   6·55 ,,   ,,   ,, Q

If the READ list of variables had been reversed:

```
        READ (2, 30) Q, VOLTS, AMPS
```

then the value 16·1 would have been assigned to Q
                300·0   ,,   ,,   ,,   ,,   ,, VOLTS
                 6·55   ,,   ,,   ,,   ,,   ,, AMPS

Integer input

When integer numbers are to be read into the computer, each integer number occupying a field is coded separately according to the formula:

$$Iw$$

where I—is the code for an integer;
       w—is the field width (as for real numbers).

Consider the integers 16 and 3966 positioned on the data card as follows:

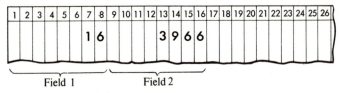

1	2	3	4	5	6	7	8	9	10	11	12	13	14	15	16	17	18	19	20	21	22	23	24	25	26
						1	6					3	9	6	6										

       Field 1   Field 2

The number in field 1 is coded I8 and the number in field 2 is coded I8.

The FORMAT statement describing this data card can therefore be written as:

```
10 FORMAT (I8, I8)
```

or more concisely
```
10 FORMAT (2I8)
```

assuming the statement is to be numbered 10.

Example 2

Read the three numbers 10, 3000 and 100 from the following data card and assign these values to the integer variables MIN, MAX, INC.

1	2	3	4	5	6	7	8	9	10	11	12	13	14	15	16	17	18	19	20	21	22	23	24	25	26
				1	0				3	0	0	0				1	0	0							

A suitable pair of input statements for this data would be:

```
     READ (2,100) MIN, MAX, INC
100 FORMAT (3I6)
```

Mixed data

Integer and real data may appear on the same data card as below:

1	2	3	4	5	6	7	8	9	10	11	12	13	14	15	16	17	18	19	20	21	22	23	24	25	26
					2	1				3	6	1	.	5	2					1	9	9			

A suitable pair of input statements for this data would be:

```
    READ (2, 55) JACK, AND, JILL
55 FORMAT (I8, F8.2, I8)
```

where JACK, JILL are integer variables and AND is a real variable.

28

Output

Any variables, integer or real, which have been used in the program (that is, defined) can be printed out on the line printer. Suppose that the real variable ANS has been assigned the value 216·913 and it is required to print out this answer. An appropriate pair of output statements would be:

```
           WRITE (3, 40) ANS
        40 FORMAT (10X, F9.3)
```

When information has to be printed out by the computer, two statements are always required (i) a WRITE statement and (ii) a FORMAT statement.

The WRITE statement

(1) The elements of the statement are as follows:

WRITE is always used at the beginning of every output statement.

3 is the unit number of the line printer. Since 'writing' can be accomplished on a variety of output devices, each one is allocated a unit number.

40 is the arbitrary number chosen for the accompanying FORMAT statement.

ANS is the variable from which data is to be printed on the line printer.

(2) The brackets and commas that appear in the WRITE statement are important.

(3) The list of variables that appears after the brackets can contain as many variables as are required, provided that these variables have been defined (that is, assigned values) in the program. These variables must be separated by commas.

Generalising, all WRITE statements must be written as specified below:

```
WRITE (Unit no., Format no.) List of variables
                             separated by commas
```

The FORMAT statement

Each line of the printer output contains 120 print positions which are available for positioning and printing answers and text:

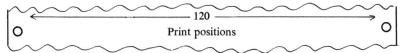

The FORMAT statement, when used in conjunction with a WRITE statement, specifies the type of numbers to be printed and their positions on the printed page. As with input formatting, real numbers and integer numbers are specified in the FORMAT statement by the codes $Fw.d$ and Iw respectively.

In output formatting the w specifies the number of print positions to be made available for the value of the variable to be outputted. Thus, w again specifies field width, but this time it refers to print positions as opposed to the card columns used in input formatting.

It is usual to request at least three more print positions than the expected number required:

(a) One for the printing of a decimal point.

(b) One for the printing of a possible negative sign.

(c) One to make allowances for at least one blank space between consecutive numbers to be printed.

A typical FORMAT statement to accommodate the printing of an expected real 6-digit number, three digits of which are decimal places, would be:

$$\text{40 FORMAT (1X, 60X, F9.3)}$$

or more concisely   40 FORMAT (61X, F9.3)

In this statement:

$1X$ —An X is the code for a blank space in an output FORMAT statement. Thus, a $1X$ means one blank space. The first specification in *every* output FORMAT statement is a carriage control specification. The carriage controls the vertical spacing of paper to give single spacing, double spacing, and so on, as in a normal typewriter. A $1X$ at the beginning of a FORMAT statement means 'jump to a new line before printing'.

$60X$—Since this is not the first specification in the FORMAT statement, 60 blank print positions are left before printing commences.

$F9.3$—This indicates that the value to be printed is real and that 9 print positions have been allocated for printing it. The right-hand three of which these positions are reserved for the decimal portion of the printed value. This is shown diagrammatically below. Let us assume that the number to be printed from the computer's store is 216·913.

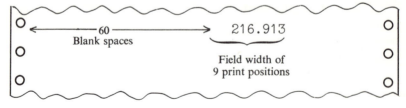

Example 3

The variables DIST and TIME are defined as 316·5 and 9·25 respectively.
Construct a suitable pair of output statements to write this out.

```
        WRITE (3, 900) DIST, TIME
    900 FORMAT (31X, F10.1, 5X, F10.2)
```

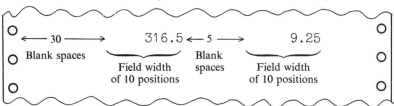

Example 4

An integer variable INCUM is to be printed (140). Construct a suitable
pair of output statements:

```
        WRITE (3,60) INCUM
    60 FORMAT (21X, I6)
```

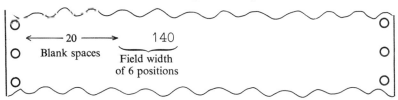

Example 5

WRITE lists can contain real and integer variables. The variables RATE,
TIME and INCUM have been assigned values of 1·5, 40·00 and 14
respectively. Construct suitable statements to write out the variables
RATE, INCUM and TIME in that order:

```
        WRITE (3, 96) RATE, INCUM, TIME
    96 FORMAT (11X, F6.1, 5X, I6, 5X, F6.2)
```

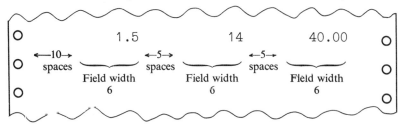

Note that the order of real and integer variables, as specified in the
WRITE statement, is maintained in the FORMAT statement.

Assignment 2

(1) Correct those of the following READ statements which are faulty:

  (i) READ (2 10) A, B, C

  (ii) READ (2 30) X Y

  (iii) READ (2, 25), VOLTS, AMPS, Q

  (iv) READ (2, 70) X, Y

(2) Shown below are illustrations of values on data cards. Assuming a FORMAT statement number of 30, write down a suitable FORMAT statement for each.

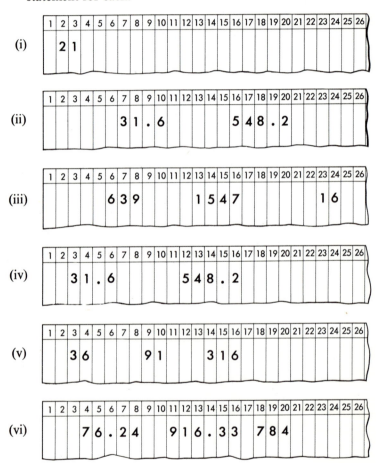

(3) Write down a suitable pair of input statements to read the data from the following data cards.

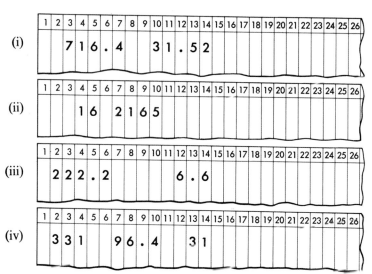

(4) In each of the examples below are shown a pair of valid input statements. The values to be assigned to the stated variables are also shown. Place the values on a data card like this:

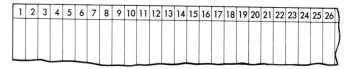

so as to comply with the input statements:

(i)   READ (2, 40) A, B, C
     40 FORMAT (3F8.1)

where A is to be assigned the value 16·2
     B ,, ,, ,,   ,,   ,,   ,, 316·4
     C ,, ,, ,,   ,,   ,,   ,,   91·2

(ii)   READ (2, 60) NI, J, K
     60 FORMAT (3I6)

where NI is to be assigned the value 25
     K ,, ,, ,,   ,,   ,,   ,, 300
     J ,, ,, ,,   ,,   ,,   ,, 700

(iii)   READ (2, 10) N, A, B
     10 FORMAT (I4, 2F9.2)

where A is to be assigned the value 24·33
     B ,, ,, ,,   ,,   ,,   ,, 916·25
     N ,, ,, ,,   ,,   ,,   ,,   6

(iv)   READ (2, 25) A, I, K, T
    25 FORMAT (F4.2, 2I4, F4.1)

where K is to be assigned the value 12

    A ,, ,, ,,   ,,   ,,   ,,   6·25

    T ,, ,, ,,   ,,   ,,   ,,   19·1

    I ,, ,, ,,   ,,   ,,   ,,   6

(5) Construct suitable WRITE statements to print the variables below in the order stated. Assume that the FORMAT statement number is 40.

(i) A B C I

(ii) PAY HOURS

(6) Correct only those of the following WRITE statements that have faulty syntax.

(i) WRITE (3, 10), A, B, C

(ii) WRITE (3.70) ANS

(iii) WRITE (3 33) AVE, A, I

(iv) WRITE (3, 9999) X, A, T

(7) How many actual print positions are used by the following FORMAT statements?

(i)   10 FORMAT (1X, F10.2)

(ii) 131 FORMAT (20X, F10.2)

(iii) 65 FORMAT (20X, 2F10.2)

(iv)   9 FORMAT (20X, F10.2, 5X, I6)

(8) Using the WRITE statements below and given that the values assigned to A, B and I are 124·0, 160·5 and 17 respectively, draw output diagrams for the following to show blank spacing and fields.

          WRITE (3, 60) B, A, I

(i) 60 FORMAT (21X, 2F10.1, I10)

(ii) 60 FORMAT (30X, 2F6.1, I8)

(iii) 60 FORMAT (30X, F6.1, 5X, F6.1, 5X, I8)

(iv) 60 FORMAT (50X, 2F8.1, 12X, I6)

(9) Correct the WRITE statements in each of the examples below, assuming that in each case the FORMAT statement is correct,

(i)   WRITE (3, 20) A, C, D
      30 FORMAT (1X, F10.2, 3X, F10.2, 3X, F10.2)

(ii)   WRITE (3, 44) A, I, D
      44 FORMAT (1X, F10.2, 3X, F10.2, 3X, I10)

34

(10) Assuming that the WRITE statements and the field widths in the FORMAT statements are correct, state what is still wrong with each of the following FORMAT statements. Rectify the FORMAT statements accordingly.

(i)
```
      WRITE (3, 300) A, I, C
300 FORMAT (30X, I6, 2X, F10.2, 2X, F10.2)
```

(ii)
```
      WRITE (3, 100) A, B, I, F
100 FORMAT (20X, I6, 3F10.2)
```

Practical Session 3
Averaging Two Real Numbers

Consider a program to read two real numbers into the computer, calculate their average, and print out the result.

A simple flowchart, which helps to summarise the steps involved in the program, is given below.

Flowchart for program 1:

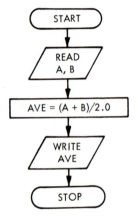

Remember that the numbers to be read into the computer as data can be positioned anywhere on the data card. It is therefore decided to position the two real numbers 21·600 and 315·584 on the data card as shown below:

1	2	3	4	5	6	7	8	9	10	11	12	13	14	15	16	17	18	19	20	21	22	23	24	25	26
				2	1	.	6	0	0				3	1	5	.	5	8	4						

The formatting of this data card is given by:

$$\text{FORMAT (2F10.3)}$$

Fortran coding for program:

```
// JOB T
// FOR
*LIST SOURCE PROGRAM
*IOCS(CARD, 1132 PRINTER)
```

```
C       PROGRAM TO FIND THE AVERAGE OF TWO REAL
C       NUMBERS
        READ (2, 10) A, B
   10 FORMAT (2F10.3)
        AVE = (A + B)/2.0
        WRITE (3, 20) AVE
   20 FORMAT (20X, F10.3)
        CALL EXIT
        END
// XEQ
      21.600    315.584
```

Printer output:

168.592

Analysing Program 1

All instructions are executed in the order in which they are presented on the coding sheet, that is, the order in which they appear in the source program deck.

`// JOB T`

Purpose: To initiate the computer for a new program which is about to follow.

`// FOR`

Purpose: To call the appropriate compiler into action, in this case the Fortran compiler.

`*LIST SOURCE PROGRAM`

Purpose: To tell the Fortran compiler to print a copy of the source program instructions on the printer output.

`*IOCS(CARD, 1132 PRINTER)`

Purpose: To notify the compiler that use of the card reader and the line printer will be required during the execution of the program.

`C PROGRAM TO FIND THE AVERAGE OF TWO REAL`
`C NUMBERS`

Purpose: To provide a facility for comments to be included as part of the source listing. These comment cards take no part in the actual execution of the program.

37

READ (2, 10) A, B

Purpose: To cause information to be read from the card reader and assigned to the two variables *A* and *B*.

10 FORMAT (2F10.3)

Purpose: To provide the READ statement above with the necessary information regarding the type of data to be found and its position on the data card.

AVE = (A + B)/2.0

Purpose: To instruct the computer to add the assigned values of *A* and *B*, divide this sum by 2·0 and assign the result to the variable AVE.

WRITE (3, 20) AVE

Purpose: To cause information to be printed on the line printer, in this case the value assigned to the variable AVE by the previous instruction.

20 FORMAT (20X, F10.3)

Purpose: To provide the WRITE statement with the necessary information regarding the type of data to be printed and its whereabouts on the printer output.

CALL EXIT

Purpose: To cause the computer to terminate the program and start on the next program if there is one, that is, look for another // JOB T card.

END

Purpose: This statement notifies the compiler that it has come to the last Fortran instruction, whereupon it should proceed with compilation (that is, translation from Fortran into machine language) and checking for errors in syntax.

// XEQ

Purpose: To initiate execution of the program which has just been compiled and found to be free of errors. Execution then begins with the first executable statement in the program, in this case the READ statement.

21.600   315.584

Purpose: To provide the data which the READ statement requires.

From a careful reading of the above analysis it can be seen that a program is a set of sequential operations, each one being carried to completion before the next is initiated. All jobs presented to the computer must be broken down into a set of sequential instructions. If a job cannot be broken down in this way, then the computer cannot do it.

Output Labelling

Let us consider now a method of supplying the single numerical result provided by the computer as output to the previous program with a label.

Text quotes can be used to supply informative labels to the output from of a program. They are single quotation marks enclosing the desired label. This text material is inserted into the FORMAT statement associated with the appropriate WRITE statement, in the position in which it is required in the output. For example, an informative label printed before the average might be:

```
THE AVERAGE OF THE TWO NUMBERS IS.......
```

FORMAT statement 20 in the previous program would be modified as shown below:

```
20 FORMAT (20X, 'THE AVERAGE OF THE TWO
                   NUMBERS IS', F10.3)
```

Text material may appear any number of times in a FORMAT statement. If the two data values read from the data card, as well as their average were to be printed, a useful label for insertion into the FORMAT statement would be:

```
THE AVERAGE OF.......AND.......IS.......
```

The modified FORMAT and WRITE statements would now appear as:

```
   WRITE (3, 20) A, B, AVE
20 FORMAT (20X, 'THE AVERAGE OF', F10.3, ' AND',
                   F10.3, ' IS', F10.3)
```

(See Appendix A for an equivalent way of writing this FORMAT statement.)

The previous program 1, modified to include informative labels, is rewritten below as program 2.

Coding for program 2:

```
// JOB T
// FOR
*LIST SOURCE PROGRAM
*IOCS(CARD, 1132 PRINTER)
C      PROGRAM TO DEMONSTRATE THE LABELLING
C      OF OUTPUT
```

(Continued overleaf . . .)

```
      READ(2, 10) A, B
   10 FORMAT (2F10.3)
      AVE = (A + B)/2.0
      WRITE (3, 20) A, B, AVE
   20 FORMAT (20X, 'THE AVERAGE OF', F10.3, ' AND',
                           F10.3, ' IS', F10.3)
      CALL EXIT
      END
// XEQ
   21.600    315.584
```

Printer output:

```
THE AVERAGE OF 21.600 AND 315.584 IS 168.592
```

Instruction Looping

Finding the average of two numbers by writing a program appears to be somewhat pointless, since it could have been calculated manually in a much shorter time. In fact, nobody would use a computer to do just this, but if the averages of hundreds or even thousands of pairs of numbers were required, then a computer would be used, since each average would be calculated with the same great speed and unfailing accuracy.

The program to find the average of two real numbers can, by the addition of one new instruction, become a very powerful program indeed, capable of averaging many number pairs. This new instruction is the GO TO instruction, shown in its general form below:

$$\boxed{\text{GO TO } n}$$

where n is the number of a statement elsewhere in the program.

By placing a number after the TO, in the GO TO . . . instruction, the computer can be made to jump unconditionally to the statement whose number is quoted, regardless of where that instruction appears in the program. Thus, this instruction GO TO 300 would send the computer to statement 300, which the computer would then execute. Having executed statement 300, it would carry on in sequence until it met that GO TO instruction again or some other GO TO instruction.

Taking advantage of the GO TO instruction, it is possible to make the computer execute the same program instructions again and again indefinitely. This is called *looping*.

40

Consider program 1 now modified to deal with many data cards, each having a pair of real numbers punched on it and complying with the FORMAT requirements used previously. A flowchart for the new program 3 is given below.

Flowchart for program 3:

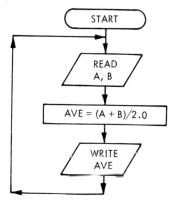

Coding for program 3:

```
// JOB T
// FOR
*LIST SOURCE PROGRAM
*IOCS(CARD, 1132 PRINTER)
C      PROGRAM TO CALCULATE MANY AVERAGES
   300 READ (2, 10) A, B
    10 FORMAT (2F10.3)
       AVE = (A + B)/2.0
       WRITE (3, 20) A, B, AVE
    20 FORMAT (20X, 'THE AVERAGE OF', F10.3, ' AND',
                        F10.3, ' IS', F10.3)
       GO TO 300
       END
// XEQ
    21.600    315.584
   101.230     56.340
   220.400     50.500
     1.080      9.090
```

Printer output:

```
THE AVERAGE OF  21.600 AND 315.584 IS 168.592
THE AVERAGE OF 101.230 AND  56.340 IS  78.785
THE AVERAGE OF 220.400 AND  50.500 IS 135.450
THE AVERAGE OF   1.080 AND   9.090 IS   5.085
```

Note

(1) Instructions are obeyed in sequence unless the computer is directed by means of a GO TO instruction to do otherwise. Each time the computer is directed to statement 300, sequential instruction execution is again carried out.

(2) The first time the READ instruction is executed, the values assigned to A and B are those to be found on the first data card, i.e. 21·600 and 315·584 respectively. The second time the READ instruction is executed, the values assigned to A and B are those of the second data card, i.e. 101·230 and 56·340 respectively, and so on.

(3) Because the values assigned to A and B change with each pass through the loop of instructions, the value assigned to the variable AVE in the arithmetic statement also changes.

(4) The WRITE statement simply prints the changing values assigned to A, B and AVE with each pass through the loop.

Counting

It has already been shown in Practical Session 1 that if the instruction:

$$\text{KOUNT} = \text{KOUNT} + 1$$

is repeatedly executed, the effect will be to add 1 to the variable KOUNT each time.

Consider now how a counting routine can be built into the endless loop program so that a printed statement of which data card is being processed, is included in the print-out.

Coding for general approach:

```
      KOUNT = 0                    —initialise
300   READ (2, 10) A, B
 10   FORMAT (2F10.3)
      KOUNT = KOUNT + 1            —increment
      (Other program statements)
      WRITE (3, 30) KOUNT          —print
 30   FORMAT (20X, 'DATA CARD NUMBER', I4)

      (Other program statements)

      GO TO 300
```

Flowchart for general approach:

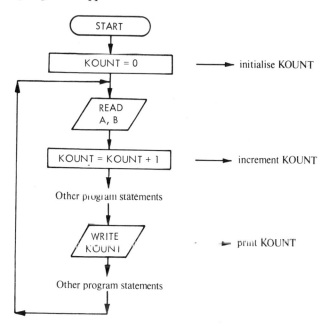

Note

(1) It is essential to initialise any counters or accumulators in a program. Do not assume that the computer will automatically do this, because it will not. Initialisation is always performed at the start of a program.

(2) The statement KOUNT = 0 is executed only once. If it were included within the loop of instructions, it would set KOUNT to zero each time the loop was performed.

(3) The first time through the loop of instructions, KOUNT will be assigned the value 1. The WRITE statement will print out the current value of KOUNT according to the specifications in FORMAT statement 30. The second time through the loop, KOUNT is assigned the value 2, and so on.

(4) Counting is performed in integer mode, and this fact is duly taken into account in FORMAT statement 20, where I4 is the output field specification for KOUNT.

The original program 1 is now modified to contain the features outlined above, and becomes program 4, which is shown overleaf.

Flowchart for program 4:

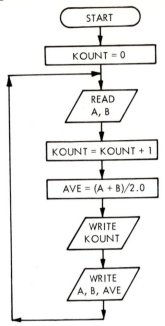

Coding for program 4:

```
// JOB T
// FOR
*LIST SOURCE PROGRAM
*IOCS(CARD, 1132 PRINTER)
C      PROGRAM USING A COUNTING ROUTINE
       KOUNT = 0
  300 READ (2, 10) A, B
   10 FORMAT (2F10.3)
       KOUNT = KOUNT + 1
       AVE = (A + B)/2.0
       WRITE (3, 30) KOUNT
   30 FORMAT (20X, 'DATA CARD NUMBER', I4)
       WRITE (3, 20) A, B, AVE
   20 FORMAT (20X, 'THE AVERAGE OF', F10.3,' AND',
                               F10.3,' IS', F10.3)

       GO TO 300
       END
// XEQ
      21.600    315.584
     101.230     56.340
     220.400     50.500
       1.080      9.090
```

Printer output:

```
DATA CARD NUMBER 1
THE AVERAGE OF   21.600 AND 315.584 IS 168.592
DATA CARD NUMBER 2
THE AVERAGE OF 101.230 AND  56.340 IS  78.785
DATA CARD NUMBER 3
THE AVERAGE OF 220.400 AND  50.500 IS 135.450
DATA CARD NUMBER 4
THE AVERAGE OF    1.080 AND   9.090 IS   5.085
```

Note

(1) This program demonstrates not only the COUNTING ROUTINE but also for the first time that two WRITE statements may be used in one program. In general any statement can be used as often as it is required within the confines of a single program.

(2) Because the FORMAT statements associated with the two WRITE statements each have a blank carriage control specification, a new line is taken for each of the two lines of print.

Assignment 3

(1) Write a program to find the average of three numbers read from a data card which you have formatted and print out simply the one numerical result.

(2) Write a program to find the average of four numbers read from a data card and print out not only the single answer but also a meaningful label and the four input values.

(3) Write a program to read into the computer many data cards, each containing five numbers and all of the same FORMAT specifications. Find the average of each set of values and print out the answers as well as the input values, fully labelled.

(4) Write a program to read many data cards, each containing four values, and average them. Include in your program a counting system such that the final output will contain not only a fully labelled output of answers and input values, but also a count of each and every card that has been read as input of data.

Practical Session 4
Programmed Decision Making

As was pointed out in Practical Session 3, there is no means of exiting from a continuous loop of instructions that essentially reads a data card, calculates the average, prints out the result and then returns to read another card, calculate another average, and so on.

The discussion which follows reveals how the computer is instructed to make a decision so that it can exit automatically from the loop under various specified decision criteria. Computers cannot, of course, make decisions in the same way as we can. They can decide only if one number is bigger than or less than another or is equal to it. The most widely used decision-making statement in Fortran is the IF statement.

The IF Statement
A typical example of such a statement might be:

$$IF\ (A)\ 10,\ 20,\ 30$$

The essential features of all IF statements are:
- (a) The word IF is used.
- (b) The expression under test is enclosed in brackets.
- (c) The bracketed expression is always followed by three numbers separated by commas. These are the numbers of other statements in the program.

The operation of the IF statement automatically evaluates the expression to determine if the result is (a) negative, (b) zero or (c) positive. The actual numerical value does not matter, it is only the sign or a zero that is important. In the above IF statement:
- (a) If A is found *negative*, the next statement to be executed is 10.
- (b) If A is found *zero*, the next statement to be executed is 20.
- (c) If A is found *positive*, the next statement to be executed is 30.

Because of the ability of the IF statement to make the computer jump to any one of three possible points in the program, the IF statement is often called a three-way decision-making statement. A two-way decision is also possible using the IF statement. It is accomplished by making two of the required three statement numbers the same. Which two are made the same depends on the requirements to be met by the statement.

e.g. $$IF\ (A)\ 20,\ 20,\ 30$$

If A is either negative or zero, the jump is made to statement 20, otherwise, if A is positive, the jump is made to statement 30.

Expressions enclosed within brackets can be as complex as the situations demand, the only restriction placed upon them is that they should not be of mixed mode.

Example 1

A counting system within a program may require the use of an IF statement to jump automatically out of the loop when KOUNT has reached the value 10, say:

```
IF (10 - KOUNT) 60, 60, 90.
```

where statement 60 is CALL EXIT.

Note that if KOUNT started with a value of zero and was being incremented by 1, (10 − KOUNT) would never become negative, since statement 60 would be executed when the expression became zero. Under these conditions three statement numbers are still required but it does not matter which of the two statement numbers the impossible case is made equal to.

Example 2

An IF statement can be used to determine whether or not the roots of a quadratic equation are imaginary or not:

```
IF (B**2 - 4.0*A*C) 200, 300, 200
```

where statement 200 may be a WRITE statement to print the words 'roots imaginary'.

The IF statement can be summed up in general terms as follows:

IF (Expression)	n_1	, n_2	, n_3
	if negative	if zero	if positive

Terminating a Program as a Result of a Decision

The general structure of a program which is required to process ten data cards and then terminate is shown below:

```
    KOUNT = 0
300 READ (2, 10) A, B
 10 FORMAT (2F10.3)
    KOUNT = KOUNT + 1
    IF (10 - KOUNT) 66, 33, 33
 33 AVE = (A + B)/2.0

    (other program statements)

    GO TO 300
 66 CALL EXIT
```

Note

(1) The IF statement is a two-way decision-making statement. Either the program goes on to calculate AVE (statement number 33) or it exits from the loop (statement number 66), depending on the value of (10 — KOUNT).

(2) As long as KOUNT ≤ 10, statement 33 is executed in response to the IF statement.

(3) As soon as KOUNT > 10, statement 66 is executed in response to the IF statement.

(4) Eleven data cards are actually read by the computer before the program is terminated. But in the case of the eleventh card no average is calculated and no results are printed, since these instructions are bypassed.

The flowchart given in Practical Session 3 can now be redrawn as shown below, to take account of the automatic exit from the program after the tenth data card has been processed.

Flowchart for program:

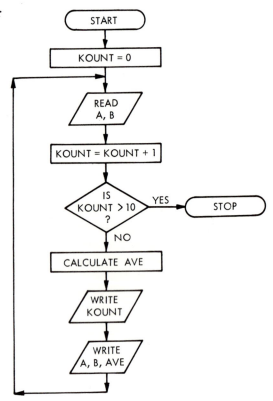

Coding for program:

```
// JOB T
// FOR
*LIST SOURCE PROGRAM
*IOCS(CARD, 1132 PRINTER)
C       PROGRAM WHICH AUTOMATICALLY STOPS
C       AFTER PROCESSING TEN DATA CARDS
        KOUNT = 0
  300 READ(2, 10) A, B
   10 FORMAT (2F10.3)
        KOUNT = KOUNT + 1
        IF (10 - KOUNT) 66, 33, 33
   33 AVE = (A + B)/2.0
        WRITE (3, 30) KOUNT
   30 FORMAT (20X, 'DATA CARD NUMBER', I4)
        WRITE (3, 20) A, B, AVE
   20 FORMAT (20X, 'THE AVERAGE OF', F10.3, ' AND',
                         F10.3, ' IS', F10.3)
        GO TO 300
   66 CALL EXIT
        END
// XEQ
      21.600      315.584
     101.230       56.340
     220.400       50.500
       1.080        9.090
    1000.001      316.441
       1.204        6.542
      99.106      100.002
      36.501       94.653
     311.053      102.455
       1.200        3.060
     150.000      140.000
      24.151       66.222
```

(The printer output is shown overleaf.)

Printer output:

```
DATA CARD NUMBER 1
THE AVERAGE OF   21.600 AND 315.584 IS 168.592
DATA CARD NUMBER 2
THE AVERAGE OF 101.230 AND  56.340 IS  78.785
DATA CARD NUMBER 3
THE AVERAGE OF 220.400 AND  50.500 IS 135.450
DATA CARD NUMBER 4
THE AVERAGE OF    1.080 AND   9.090 IS   5.085
DATA CARD NUMBER 5
THE AVERAGE OF1000.001 AND 316.441 IS 658.221
DATA CARD NUMBER 6
THE AVERAGE OF    1.204 AND   6.542 IS   3.873
DATA CARD NUMBER 7
THE AVERAGE OF   99.106 AND 100.002 IS  99.554
DATA CARD NUMBER 8
THE AVERAGE OF   36.501 AND  94.653 IS  65.577
DATA CARD NUMBER 9
THE AVERAGE OF 311.053 AND 102.455 IS 206.254
DATA CARD NUMBER 10
THE AVERAGE OF    1.200 AND   3.060 IS   2.130
```

Note

(1) Although there are twelve data cards shown as input, only the first ten have been processed as expected.

(2) Other suitable IF statements that could have achieved the same end as the one used in the program are:

    (*a*)   IF (KOUNT - 10) 33, 33, 66
    (*b*)   IF (11 - KOUNT) 66, 66, 33
    (*c*)   IF (KOUNT - 11) 33, 66, 66

A More General Program

Programs should always be written so that they are as general as possible. For example, the previous program has built into it a checking device, in the form of an IF statement, to stop the program after ten data cards have been processed. For this reason, it is only suitable for processing ten data cards. For processing, say, one hundred data cards, part of the program would have to be rewritten.

One way of making the program able to cope with varying numbers of data cards would be to include within the IF statement a variable instead of the constant 10. This variable could then be assigned a value by reading it from a data card. The flowchart and part program following show this technique.

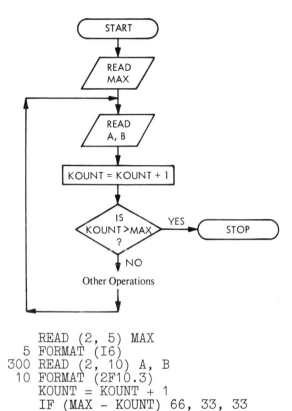

```
      READ (2, 5) MAX
    5 FORMAT (I6)
  300 READ (2, 10) A, B
   10 FORMAT (2F10.3)
      KOUNT = KOUNT + 1
      IF (MAX - KOUNT) 66, 33, 33
```
(Other program statements)
```
      GO TO 300
```

Thus the value of MAX is read from the first data card, and this READ statement is not executed again, otherwise MAX would change in value each time the loop was executed. Thus to alter the number of data cards that the program should process each time it is used, all that need be done is to supply a first data card, punched in the appropriate field with the maximum number of data cards required.

Last card technique

Another simple, but effective technique of writing a more general program is to use the *last card technique*. This requires the use of a special card as the last data card of the deck, say, a card punched with a negative number. Each time a data card is read into the computer, it is checked by the program to see whether or not it contains this particular negative number. If it is found to have this number, the program is halted. If not, the program continues.

Example 3

Let us consider a program to illustrate the last card technique. We shall use the previous program, but this time we shall insert into the data deck a card punched with $-1{\cdot}000$ in field one to act as a last card. (It is assumed that no legal data will have this particular value.)

Flowchart for program:

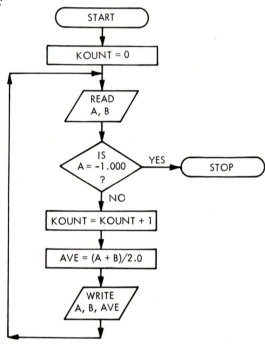

Coding for program:

```
// JOB T
// FOR
*LIST SOURCE PROGRAM
*IOCS(CARD, 1132 PRINTER)
C      PROGRAM TO DEMONSTRATE THE
C      LAST CARD TECHNIQUE
       KOUNT = 0
  300 READ (2, 10) A, B
   10 FORMAT (2F10.3)
       IF (-1.000 - A) 60, 40, 60
   60 KOUNT = KOUNT + 1
       AVE = (A + B)/2.0
       WRITE (3, 30) KOUNT
   30 FORMAT (20X, 'DATA CARD NUMBER', I4)
       WRITE (3, 20) A, B, AVE
```

```
 20 FORMAT (20X, 'THE AVERAGE OF', F10.3, ' AND',
                              F10.3, ' IS', F10.3)
    GO TO 300
 40 CALL EXIT
    END
// XEQ
    21.600      315.584
   101.230       56.340
    -1.000
```

Printer output:

```
  DATA CARD NUMBER 1
O THE AVERAGE OF  21.600 AND 315.584 IS  168.592  O
  DATA CARD NUMBER 2
O THE AVERAGE OF 101.230 AND  56.340 IS   78.785  O
```

Note that it is only when the card containing −1·000 is encountered that the program will be brought to a halt. So the end card can have as many cards in front of it as we wish. This means that we have a more general program than we had previously. There is no need to change any part of the program to deal with different numbers of data cards. All that has to be done is to make sure that the special 'end' card has been included as the last physical card in the data deck. It also means that the actual number of data cards need not be known.

Example 4

By way of a change from finding the average of two numbers, let us consider a somewhat improbable situation in which the G.P.O. decide to run an advertising campaign. To attract attention to their campaign, they decide to give to any subscriber with a winning telephone number 100 free calls.

Let us assume that the G.P.O. have a card file containing each subscriber's telephone number. Each number is an all numeric number consisting of a three-digit number followed by a four-digit number. Each telephone number is on a separate card, which is punched so that the three-digit number is located in the first six-card columns and the four-digit number is located in the next six card columns, as below:

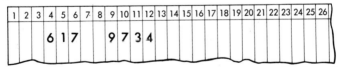

It is decided that any telephone number which has its four-digit number numerically four times the value of its three-digit number will be deemed a winning number.

53

The requirements of the problem are:

(*a*) Find all the winning numbers and print them.

(*b*) Count and print the total number of winning numbers.

(*c*) Count and print the total number of subscribers.

(*d*) Calculate and print the percentage winning numbers.

Note that, since there are always new subscribers being added to the file the exact number of subscribers at any given instant is not known. We shall therefore use the last card technique and count the total number of cards as in the last example. A possible flowchart of the program follows.

Flowchart for program:

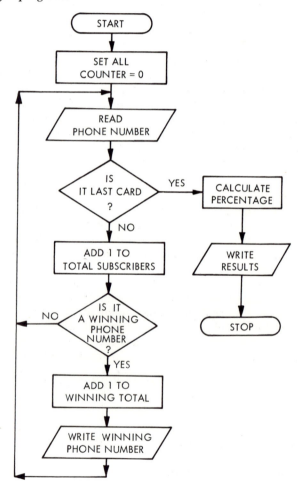

Let LTOT and LWIN be the total number of subscribers and the winning number of subscribers respectively. Also let M be the first three digits and N be the last four digits of the telephone number.

Coding for program:

```
// JOB T
// FOR
*LIST SOURCE PROGRAM
*IOCS(CARD, 1132 PRINTER)
C     PROGRAM TO DETERMINE WINNING
C     TELEPHONE NUMBERS
      LTOT = 0
      LWIN = 0
  200 READ (2, 10) M, N
   10 FORMAT (2I6)
      IF (M) 400, 500, 500
  500 LTOT = LTOT + 1
      IF (N - 4*M) 200, 700, 200
  700 LWIN = LWIN + 1
      WRITE (3, 20) M, N
   20 FORMAT (10X,'A WINNING TELEPHONE NUMBER',2I6)
      GO TO 200
  400 WRITE (3, 30) LTOT, LWIN
   30 FORMAT (10X, 'THE TOTAL NUMBER OF
                         SUBSCRIBERS IS', I6,
     1'THE NUMBER OF WINNING SUBSCRIBERS IS', I6)
      TOTAL = LTOT
      TOTWN = LWIN
      PERCE = TOTWN/TOTAL*100.0
      WRITE (3, 40) PERCE
   40 FORMAT (10X, 'PERCENTAGE WINNING
                         SUBSCRIBERS IS', F10.2)
      CALL EXIT
      END
// XEQ
   214  6789
   313  1252
   691  1234
   678  2712
   333  1665
    -1
```

Printer output:

```
A WINNING TELEPHONE NUMBER  313  1252
A WINNING TELEPHONE NUMBER  678  2712
THE TOTAL NUMBER OF SUBSCRIBERS IS 5
          THE NUMBER OF WINNING SUBSCRIBERS IS 2
PERCENTAGE WINNING SUBSCRIBERS IS 40.00
```

Note

(1) Two separate counters are required. One is used for the total number of subscribers and the other for the total number of winning subscribers. It is impossible to use the same counter for both.

(2) Since telephone numbers are integers, integer variables have been chosen, i.e. M and N. The two counters are counting integral quantities and are thus integer variables, i.e. LTOT and LWIN.

(3) The check for the lucky number has been incorporated into the IF statement which has been reproduced below for inspection.

```
IF (N - 4*M) 200, 700, 200
```

i.e. we are checking to find out if N = 4*M, or to put it another way, if N − 4*M = 0. In the above IF statement it is only when the quantity in brackets is equal to zero that the program will go to statement number 700 and add one to the winning count.

(4) Since the 'percentage calculation' will possibly involve decimal places (because division is used), it is required to change the integer variables LTOT and LWIN into real variables, say, TOTAL and TOTWN in order to do the calculation.

(5) There are two decisions to be made during this program:
(a) Has the last card been read?   (b) Is the card a winning card?
Because there are two decisions, we require two IF statements.

Assignment 4

(1) Write a program to read into the computer only six data cards, each containing four real numbers. Calculate the average of the four numbers on each data card and print out the answers, together with the input values. Label your outputs.

(2) Write a program using the last card technique to read into the computer the same data cards as in the above program. Calculate the averages again and print out the results, together with a card count. Ensure that you have at least 10 data cards for this program.

(3) Write a program to read into the computer many data cards, each containing two real numbers. Decide which of the two numbers in each case is the greater and print this out, together with the two input values, fully labelled in some meaningful fashion.

(4) Write a program to read into the computer many data cards, each containing three real numbers. Decide which of the three is the biggest and print this out, together with the input values. Label your outputs fully.

(5) Write a program which reads two of the angles of a triangle from a data card and prints out a message to the effect that the triangle is equiangular or isosceles.

Practical Session 5
Programming and Tabulation

You have probably begun to appreciate that the computer can handle and process large amounts of data. In the course of this session we are going to look at the tabulation aspects of computing.

The computer can produce large quantities of tabulated values. Most tabulation problems make use of a counting system of one type or another. Other essential requirements are that a starting value, a final value, and an incremental value must be specified. If there were no starting value, the problem would never begin. If there were no final value, the program would never terminate. If there were no incremental value, the program would immediately terminate after the first result had been tabulated.

To initialise, increment and terminate, we use a counting system, as introduced in Practical Session 3, together with an IF statement to test for the final value of the count. The general structure of the program could be like this:

KOUNT = 0   —initialise
(Other program statements)
KOUNT = KOUNT + 1   —increment
(Other program statements)
IF (TEST − KOUNT)n_1, n_2, n_3 —test

where TEST is the final value of KOUNT and n_1, n_2, and n_3 are other statement numbers in the program to which control will pass, depending on the value of (TEST − KOUNT).

Tables of tabulated values are used each day in such forms as a Ready Reckoner, which contains among other things conversion tables of one quantity to another, or mathematical tables.

Example 1
Program 1: A program is required to construct a conversion table from new pence to old pence. The constraints placed upon the program are:
(a) It must begin with zero new pence.
(b) It must finish at ten new pence.

(*c*) It must increment by one new penny at a time.

(*d*) It must produce an output in the form shown below:

$$\ldots \text{OLD PENCE} = \ldots \text{NEW PENCE}$$

Since 2·4 old pence are the equivalent of 1 new penny, then a formula for the conversion of new pence into old pence might be written as:

$$\text{PENCO} = 2.4 * \text{PENCN} + 0.005$$

where PENCO and PENCN are the real variables containing old pence and new pence respectively. The 0·005 rounds all calculated values for PENCO to two decimal places. A suitable flowchart for the conversion program, which we shall term program 1, is given below.

Flowchart for program 1:

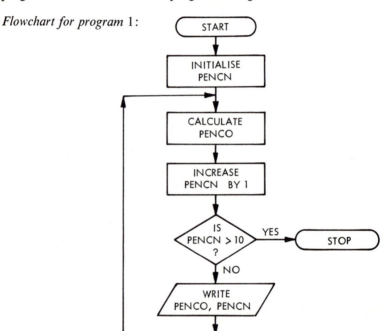

Coding for program 1:

```
// JOB T
// FOR
*LIST SOURCE PROGRAM
*IOCS(CARD, 1132 PRINTER)
C     PROGRAM TO CONVERT NEW PENCE
C     TO OLD PENCE
      PENCN = 0.
  300 PENCO = 2.4 * PENCN + 0.005
      WRITE (3, 40) PENCO, PENCN
```

58

```
   40 FORMAT (20X, F5.2, ' OLD PENCE = ', F4.0,
                                   ' NEW PENCE')
      PENCN = PENCN + 1.
      IF (10. - PENCN) 500, 300, 300
  500 CALL EXIT
      END
// XEQ
```

Printer output:

```
          0.00  OLD  PENCE  =  0.  NEW  PENCE
          2.40  OLD  PENCE  =  1.  NEW  PENCE
          4.80  OLD  PENCE  =  2.  NEW  PENCE
          7.20  OLD  PENCE  =  3.  NEW  PENCE
          9.60  OLD  PENCE  =  4.  NEW  PENCE
         12.00  OLD  PENCE  =  5.  NEW  PENCE
         14.40  OLD  PENCE  =  6.  NEW  PENCE
         16.80  OLD  PENCE  =  7.  NEW  PENCE
         19.20  OLD  PENCE  =  8.  NEW  PENCE
         21.60  OLD  PENCE  =  9.  NEW  PENCE
         24.00  OLD  PENCE  =10.  NEW  PENCE
```

A fact about the above program that may have gone unnoticed is that it differs from all other programs that we have studied so far. This is the first program that requires no data cards to be supplied. All the data required by the program is supplied within the program itself.

Program 2: Now that we have produced a tabulated output, let us change the program slightly, such that the modified program, which we shall term program 2, will obey a new set of constraints:

(*a*) The table has to start with an initial value of five new pence.

(*b*) The table will increment in steps of ten new pence.

(*c*) The table will terminate having calculated 35 new pence.

The flowchart for program 2 is the same as that for program 1, except that some of the values in it have to be changed.

Coding for program 2:

```
// JOB T
// FOR
*LIST SOURCE PROGRAM
*IOCS(CARD, 1132 PRINTER)
C      PROGRAM TO CONVERT NEW PENCE
C      TO OLD PENCE
       PENCN = 5.
  300  PENCO = 2.4 * PENCN + 0.005
       WRITE (3, 40) PENCO, PENCN
```

(*Continued overleaf . . .*)

```
  40 FORMAT (20X, F10.2, ' OLD PENCE = ', F10.0,
                                      ' NEW PENCE')
     PENCN = PENCN + 10.
     IF (35. - PENCN) 500, 300, 300
 500 CALL EXIT
     END
// XEQ
```

Printer output:

```
     12.00 OLD PENCE =   5. NEW PENCE
     36.00 OLD PENCE =  15. NEW PENCE
     60.00 OLD PENCE =  25. NEW PENCE
     84.00 OLD PENCE =  35. NEW PENCE
```

Note the following:

(*a*) The initialisation of PENCN to 5.

$$(PENCN = 5.)$$

(*b*) The increment of 10. in PENCN

$$(PENCN = PENCN + 10.)$$

(*c*) The test for a maximum of 35. PENCN

$$(IF (35. - PENCN) 500, 300, 300)$$

It is worthy of special note that, although in the above program we are initialising and incrementing new pence, there is no reason why we cannot test for an upper limit to the number of old pence instead. For example, if we did not require the conversion table to exceed, say, 100 old pence, we need only change the IF statement to:

```
     IF (100. - PENCO) 500, 300, 300
```

Program 3: In Practical Session 4, we pointed out that it is always good programming technique to make a program as general as possible within the given framework. The conversion table we have been studying above suffers from three serious limitations:

(*a*) Its starting value is fixed.

(*b*) Its incremental value is fixed.

(*c*) Its maximum value is also fixed.

Let us now design a program, which we shall term program 3, that will give flexibility to these limitations. This is not as difficult as it may seem at first glance. In fact, all that need be done is to write the program in such a way that the different values to be assigned to the three parameters mentioned above can be read into the computer from a single data card. In effect, this means that the above limitations can be varied by changing the values on the single data card supplied.

60

Flowchart for program 3:

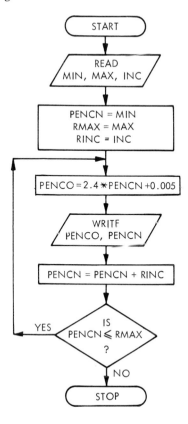

Note

(1) MAX, MIN, and INC are the integer variables for the maximum, minimum and incremental values, while PENCO and PENCN are the variables whose contents will contain old pence and new pence respectively.

(2) INC is changed in the program to RINC to keep the mode of the expression, PENCN = PENCN + RINC, in real mode. The same reasoning is applicable to RMAX.

(3) The initialising of PENCN has been accomplished by setting PENCN equal to MIN.

Coding for program 3:

```
// JOB T
// FOR
*LIST SOURCE PROGRAM
*IOCS(CARD, 1132 PRINTER)
C      CONVERSION TABLE - MORE GENERAL
       READ (2, 30) MIN, MAX, INC
    30 FORMAT (3I6)
       PENCN = MIN
       RMAX = MAX
       RINC = INC
   300 PENCO = 2.4 * PENCN + 0.005
       WRITE (3, 40) PENCO, PENCN
    40 FORMAT (20X, F5.2, ' OLD PENCE = ', F4.0,
                                  ' NEW PENCE')
       PENCN = PENCN + RINC
       IF (RMAX - PENCN) 500, 300, 300
   500 CALL EXIT
       END
// XEQ
     1    5    1
```

Printer output:

```
       2.40 OLD PENCE = 1. NEW PENCE
       4.80 OLD PENCE = 2. NEW PENCE
       7.20 OLD PENCE = 3. NEW PENCE
       9.60 OLD PENCE = 4. NEW PENCE
      12.00 OLD PENCE = 5. NEW PENCE
```

The data card in the above program contained the values 1(MIN), 5(MAX) and 1(INC). If the data card had contained the values 10(MIN), 20(MAX) and 2(INC), the printer output would have been:

```
      24.00 OLD PENCE = 10. NEW PENCE
      28.80 OLD PENCE = 12. NEW PENCE
      33.60 OLD PENCE = 14. NEW PENCE
      38.40 OLD PENCE = 16. NEW PENCE
      43.20 OLD PENCE = 18. NEW PENCE
      48.00 OLD PENCE = 20. NEW PENCE
```

Example 2

Let us consider a program for converting Fahrenheit degrees into Centigrade degrees. The formula for this conversion is as follows:

$$C = \frac{5F - 160}{9}$$

where C represents Centigrade and F represents Fahrenheit degrees.

It is required to write a program that will produce a tabulated conversion output of Fahrenheit to Centigrade degrees. All Centigrade degrees are to be rounded to two decimal places. Flexibility should be built into the program because the program could be called upon to produce a variety of tables involving different Fahrenheit ranges for conversion, with the possibility of different stepped intervals of degrees in each case.

Inspection of the conversion formula and the fact that C is required to be rounded to two decimal places implies that the calculation has to be carried out in real mode. Thus, the Fortran arithmetic statement to be used in calculation will be:

$$C = (5.0 * F - 160.0)/9.0$$

The data card containing the parameters for the minimum, maximum and incremental values, will in this instance contain real numbers so as to avoid the unnecessary assignment statements in the program. That is, the MIN, MAX and INC used in the last program will now become RMIN, RMAX and RINC and will appear in the READ statement

Flowchart for program:

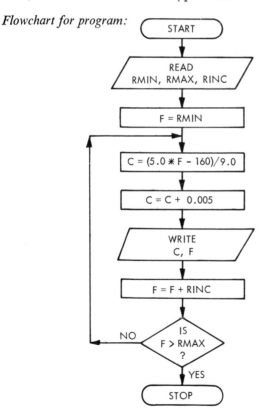

63

Coding for program:

```
// JOB T
// FOR
*LIST SOURCE PROGRAM
*IOCS(CARD, 1132 PRINTER)
C     CONVERSION FROM FAHRENHEIT TO CENTIGRADE
      READ (2, 100) RMIN, RMAX, RINC
  100 FORMAT (3F12.2)
      F = RMIN
  300 C = (5.0 * F - 160.0)/9.0
      C = C + 0.005
      WRITE (3, 200) F, C
  200 FORMAT (20X, F7.2, ' FAHRENHEIT DEGREES IS
                         THE EQUIVALENT OF', F7.2,
     1' CENTIGRADE DEGREES')
      F = F + RINC
      IF (RMAX - F) 400, 300, 300
  400 CALL EXIT
      END
// XEQ
     32.00       40.00       2.00
```

Printer output:

```
32.00 FAHRENHEIT DEGREES IS THE EQUIVALENT OF 0.00
                                        CENTIGRADE DEGREES
34.00 FAHRENHEIT DEGREES IS THE EQUIVALENT OF 1.11
                                        CENTIGRADE DEGREES
36.00 FAHRENHEIT DEGREES IS THE EQUIVALENT OF 2.22
                                        CENTIGRADE DEGREES
38.00 FAHRENHEIT DEGREES IS THE EQUIVALENT OF 3.33
                                        CENTIGRADE DEGREES
40.00 FAHRENHEIT DEGREES IS THE EQUIVALENT OF 4.44
                                        CENTIGRADE DEGREES
```

Note

(1) The conversion from Fahrenheit degrees into Centigrade degrees and the rounding of the Centigrade degrees to two decimal places have been done using two arithmetic statements. The same could have been accomplished using the one statement:

```
C = (5.0 * F - 160.0)/9.0 + 0.005
```

(2) In the above program the values chosen for the initial, final and incremental parameters were 32·00, 40·00, and 2·00. These gave five lines of output. By varying any of these parameters, the output could be extended or reduced at will.

Assignment 5

(1) Write a program which will produce a tabulated output of all the natural numbers between 1 and 50 inclusive, together with their squares and cubes.

(2) The rate of conversion from pounds sterling to dollars is 1 pound $\equiv 2\cdot377$ dollars. Produce a program which will tabulate the conversion from pounds to dollars. Your table is required to start with the conversion of one pound and end with twenty pounds.

(3) The cruising speed of the *Concorde* is designed to be about twice the speed of sound, i.e. 2390·4 km/hr. Write a program to tabulate the total distance travelled at the end of each quarter-hour interval.

(4) An electric current flowing in a conductor heats the conductor. The amount of heat generated is given by the expression:

$$H = \frac{Ri^2t}{4\cdot2}$$

where H is the heat generated in calories,
R is the resistance of the conductor in ohms,
i is the current flowing in amperes (amps),
and t is the time (seconds) for which the current flows.

Write a program to produce a table of values for H corresponding to a current which starts at 0 amps and increases to 15 amps in steps of 1 amp. Assume that t is 1 second and that R starts at 20 ohms and increases by 10 ohms for each amp rise in current.

(5) Write a program which will compute the surface area of a rectangular solid and also its volume. Assume that it starts off as a unit cube of side 1 cm. Let its length increase by 1 cm each time the surface area and volume are computed. Stop when the length reaches 20 cm. Label all output.

(6) Re-write the above program so that when a length of 20 cm is attained, the length stops increasing and the breadth begins to increase by 2 cm amounts until it reaches 40 cm. At each increment in either length or breadth the surface area and volume are computed. The height remains fixed throughout at 1 cm.

(7) Write a program to produce a tabulated output of all the natural numbers up to and including 100, together with the values of their reciprocals.

(8) Write a program which will compute and print out a table of addition facts as shown below:

$$1 + 1 = 2 \qquad\qquad 2 + 1 = 3$$
$$1 + 2 = 3 \qquad\qquad 2 + 2 = 4$$

. . . .

. . . .

. . . .

$$1 + 10 = 11 \qquad\qquad 2 + 10 = 12$$
$$3 + 1 = 4 \qquad\qquad \text{Up to: } 10 + 1 = 11$$
$$3 + 2 = 5 \qquad\qquad 10 + 2 = 12$$

. . . .

. . . .

. . . .

$$3 + 10 = 13 \qquad\qquad 10 + 10 = 20$$

Practical Session 6
Library Functions

To save the programmer a great deal of time and duplication of effort, a set of pre-written programs are supplied by the computer manufacturer with the Fortran compiler. These programs have been written so that many of the most common mathematical functions can be called by the programmer in his program. This set of supplied programs is called the *library functions*. A list of those to be studied in this Practical Session is given in the table below:

Function	Action taken by function
SQRT (X)	Computes the square root of X
SIN (X)	Computes the sine of X
COS (X)	Computes the cosine of X
ABS (X)	Computes the absolute value of X

The general structure of each of the above functions is

NAME (argument)

NAME —The name obeys the usual Fortran naming rules.

argument—This can be any arithmetic expression.

It is important to ensure that the argument is expressed in the correct units before use is made of a library function. For example, SIN and COS require in the argument to be expressed in radians, not degrees.

Using a Library Function

Consider the following examples:

```
X = SIN (C*D)
Z = COS (2.0*PI/180.0)
W = SQRT (RL/G)
A = ABS (B**2 - 4.0*A*C)
```

Note

(1) In each case the argument is enclosed by brackets.

(2) In each case the mode of the argument agrees with the function name.

(3) In each case the library function appears on the right-hand side of the '=' sign.

(4) Library functions must never be used as list elements in WRITE statements.

(5) Library functions are only used in arithmetic statements.

Example 1: SQRT(X)

Let us consider a program to tabulate WATTS, VOLT and AMPERES which will make use of one of the library functions. We shall assume that in any electrical circuit the following conditions apply:

$$V = \sqrt{W \times R}$$
$$\text{and} \quad I = V/R$$

where V is the voltage across the circuit (volts)

$\quad\quad$ I is the current flowing in the circuit (amps)

$\quad\quad$ R is the resistance of the circuit (ohms)

$\quad\quad$ W is the power in the circuit (watts)

We wish to write a program (which we shall term program 1) to produce and tabulate the calculated results of V and I as the power of the circuit, that is, W, gradually increases. R should remain fixed at 25·06 ohms.

The restrictions placed upon the program are as follows:

(*a*) The minimum, maximum and incremental values, together with the value of R, will be read into the computer (to give flexibility).

(*b*) The output is required in the following form:

(*c*) All values for WATTS are required to be rounded to four decimal places.

```
    WATTS  =  ....VOLTS  =  ....AMPERES  =  ....
    WATTS  =  ....VOLTS  =  ....AMPERES  =  ....
```

(Note in the coding for the program, opposite, that the library function SQRT computes the value of the argument and then proceeds to find the square root of it. The square root is assigned to the variable VOLTS.)

68

Flowchart for program 1:

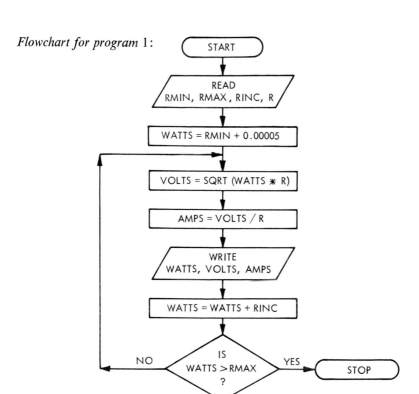

Coding for program 1:

```
// JOB T
// FOR
*LIST SOURCE PROGRAM
*IOCS(CARD, 1132 PRINTER)
C      PROGRAM DEMONSTRATES THE USE OF
C      A LIBRARY FUNCTION
       READ (2, 7) RMIN, RMAX, RINC, R
     7 FORMAT (4F10.4)
       WATTS = RMIN + 0.00005
    20 VOLTS = SQRT (WATTS/R)
       AMPS = VOLTS/R
       WRITE (3, 14) WATTS, VOLTS, AMPS
    14 FORMAT (14X, 'WATTS = ', F7.4, 4X,
          'VOLTS = ', F7.4, 4X, 'AMPERES = ',F7.4)
       WATTS = WATTS + RINC
       IF (RMAX - WATTS) 30, 20, 20
    30 CALL EXIT
       END
// XEQ
    20.0000   22.1000   0.2000    25.0600
```

Printer output:

```
○ WATTS = 20.0000   VOLTS = 22.3874 AMPERES = 0.8933 ○
  WATTS = 20.2000   VOLTS = 22.4991 AMPERES = 0.8978
○ WATTS = 20.4000   VOLTS = 22.6102 AMPERES = 0.9022 ○
  WATTS = 20.6000   VOLTS = 22.7208 AMPERES = 0.9066
○ WATTS = 20.8000   VOLTS = 22.8308 AMPERES = 0.9110 ○
  WATTS = 21.0000   VOLTS = 22.9403 AMPERES = 0.9154
○ WATTS = 21.2000   VOLTS = 23.0493 AMPERES = 0.9197 ○
  WATTS = 21.4000   VOLTS = 23.1578 AMPERES = 0.9240
  WATTS = 21.6000   VOLTS = 23.2657 AMPERES = 0.9284 ○
○ WATTS = 21.8000   VOLTS = 23.3732 AMPERES = 0.9326
  WATTS = 22.0000   VOLTS = 23.4802 AMPERES = 0.9369 ○
```

Program 2: Program 1 has demonstrated how to produce large amounts of data in tabulated form. Let us now modify program 1 so that we can include a useful heading and present the tabulated results as illustrated below:

```
○                          OHMS LAW                        ○
                 WATTS      VOLTS      AMPERES
○                  —          —           —                ○
                   —          —           —
○                  —          —           —                ○
                          and so on
```

Note how the flowchart (opposite) differs from the one for program 1. All alterations have taken place before calculation begins. If, instead of being returned to the point *X* in the flowchart, the loop had been returned to the point *Y*, then the column headings would have been printed on every alternate line of the printer output. If the loop had been returned to the point *Z*, then not only the column headings but also the main title would have been repeatedly printed.

Coding for program 2:

```
// JOB T
// FOR
*LIST SOURCE PROGRAM
*IOCS(CARD, 1132 PRINTER)
C     PROGRAM TO INTRODUCE COLUMN HEADINGS
C     AND TITLES INTO OUTPUTS
      READ (2, 7) RMIN, RMAX, RINC, R
    7 FORMAT (4F10.4)
      WRITE (3, 40)
   40 FORMAT (33X, 'OHMS LAW')
      WRITE (3, 50)
```

70

```
   50 FORMAT (21X, 'WATTS', 10X, 'VOLTS', 10X,
                                         'AMPERES')
      WATTS = RMIN + 0.00005
   20 VOLTS = SQRT (WATTS*R)
      AMPS = VOLTS/R
      WRITE (3, 14) WATTS, VOLTS  AMPS
   14 FORMAT (20X, F7.4, 8X, F7.4, 9X, F7.4)
      WATTS = WATTS + RINC
      IF (RMAX — WATTS) 30, 20, 20
   30 CALL EXIT
      END
// XEQ
   20.0000    22.1000    0.2000    25.0600
```

Flowchart for program 2:

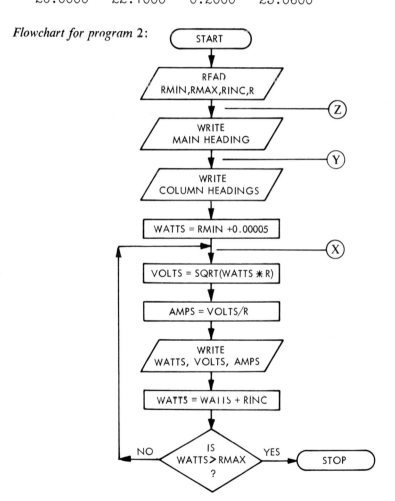

71

Printer output:

	OHMS LAW	
WATTS	VOLTS	AMPERES
20.0000	22.3874	0.8933
20.2000	22.4991	0.8978
20.4000	22.6102	0.9022
	and so on	

Program 3: The output can be further modified by 'boxing in' the table of results so that the output will appear as illustrated below:

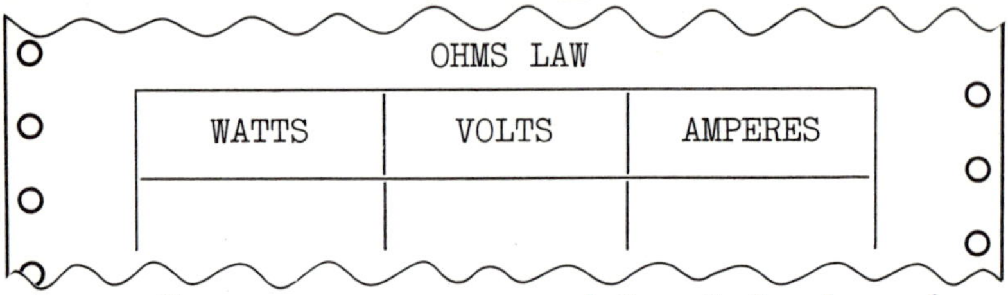

Let us call our new program, program 3. Some further changes have to be made at the beginning of the flowchart before calculation begins. The changes are shown in the part flowchart opposite.

Coding for program 3:

```
// JOB T
// FOR
*LIST SOURCE PROGRAM
*IOCS(CARD, 1132 PRINTER)
C     PROGRAM TO DEMONSTRATE BOXING OF OUTPUT
      READ (2, 7) RMIN, RMAX, RINC, R
    7 FORMAT (4F10.4)
      WRITE (3,40)
   40 FORMAT (33X, 'OHMS LAW')
      WRITE (3, 9)
    9 FORMAT (17X, '_ _ _ _ _ _ _ _ _ _ _ _ _ _
              _ _ _ _ _ _ _ _ _ _ _ _ _ _ _
              _ _ _ _ _ _ _ _ _ _ _ _ _ _-')
      WRITE (3, 10)
   10 FORMAT (17X, 'I    WATTS    I    VOLTS
                        I    AMPERES    I')
      WRITE (3, 9)
      WATTS = RMIN + 0.00005
   20 VOLTS = SQRT (WATTS*R)
      AMPS = VOLTS/R
      WRITE (3, 14) WATTS, VOLTS, AMPS
   14 FORMAT (17X, 'I', 2X, F7.4, 3X, 'I', 4X,
              F7.4, 4X, 'I', 4X, F7.4, 2X, 'I')
      WATTS = WATTS + RINC
      IF (RMAX - WATTS) 30, 20, 20
```

72

```
30 WRITE (3, 9)
   CALL EXIT
   END
// XEQ
   20.0000   22.1000   0.2000   25.0600
```

Part flowchart for program 3:

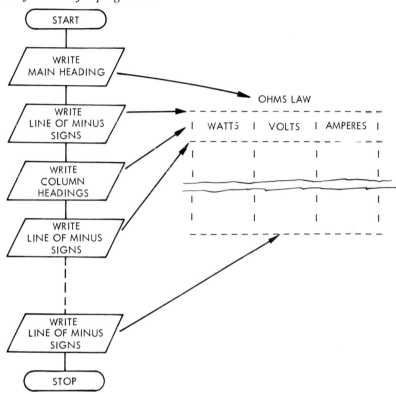

Printer output:

```
~~~~~~~~~~~~~~~~~~~~~~~~~~~~~~~~~~~~~~~~~~~~~~~~
O                     OHMS LAW                    O
  I    WATTS    I    VOLTS    I   AMPERES  I
O ----------------------------------------------- O
  I   20.0000   I   22.3874   I   0.8933   I
O I   20.2000   I   22.4991   I   0.8978   I      O
~~~~~~~~~~~~~~~~~~~~~~~~~~~~~~~~~~~~~~~~~~~~~~~~~~
  I   21.8000   I   23.3732   I   0.9326   I
O I   22.0000   I   23.4802   I   0.9369   I      O
~~~~~~~~~~~~~~~~~~~~~~~~~~~~~~~~~~~~~~~~~~~~~~~~~~
```

Note

(1) FORMAT statement number 9 is used by three different WRITE commands in the program. In other words, the same FORMAT statement can be used again and again by different WRITE statements, although the FORMAT statement itself does not immediately follow the WRITE statement which called upon it.

(2) FORMAT statement number 14 produces the body of the table. Notice how this statement has been modified to take account of the vertical division lines of the table, as has FORMAT statement 10.

Example 2: SIN(X) and COS(X)

Now we shall consider an example in using the library functions SIN(x) and COS(x). One of the basic identities in Trigonometry is stated thus:

$$\sin^2(X) + \cos^2(X) = 1$$

for any angle X degrees. Let us write a program to check that this is true. The values of X will start with $0°$ and increase in steps of $10°$ until a maximum value of $90°$ has been reached. All calculated values for the identity will be rounded to four decimal places.

Remember when using library functions such as SIN(x) and COS(x) that X must be converted to radians:

Since $180° = \pi$ radians, $X° = \dfrac{\pi \times X}{180}$ radians

Coding for program:

(In this program D stores degrees and X stores radians)

```
// JOB T
// FOR
*LIST SOURCE PROGRAM
*IOCS(CARD, 1132 PRINTER)
C      PROGRAM ILLUSTRATING USE OF LIBRARY
C      FUNCTIONS SIN(X) AND COS(X)
       WRITE (3, 10)
   10 FORMAT (20X, 'EVALUATION OF SIN(X)**2 +
                                  COS(X)**2')
       WRITE (3, 20)
   20 FORMAT (20X '- - - - - - - - - - - - - - -
              - - - - - - - - - - - - - - - -
                                  - - - - -')
       WRITE (3, 30)
   30 FORMAT (20X, 'I     DEGREES    I     FUNCTI
                                  ON    I')
       WRITE (3, 20)
       D = 0.0
       PI = 3.14
   50 X = PI*D/180.0
       Y = SIN(X)**2 + COS(X)**2 + 0.00005
```

```
        WRITE (3, 40)D, Y
  40 FORMAT (20X, 'I', F12.0, 5X, 'I', F11.4,
                                         4X, 'I')
        D = D + 10.0
        IF(90.0 - D) 60, 50, 50
  60 WRITE (3, 20)
        CALL EXIT
        END
// XEQ
```

Printer output:

```
O   EVALUATION OF SIN(X)**2 + COS(X)**2         O
    _ _ _ _ _ _ _ _ _ _ _ _ _ _ _ _ _ _ _ _
O   I     DEGREES    I     FUNCTIONS   I        O
    _ _ _ _ _ _ _ _ _ _ _ _ _ _ _ _ _ _ _ _
O   I       0.       I      1.0000     I        O
    I      10.       I      1.0000     T
    T      20.       1      1.0000     I
O   I      30.       I      1.0000     I        O
    I      40.       I      1.0000     I
O   I      50.       I      1.0000     I        O
                 and so on
O   _ _ _ _ _ _ _ _ _ _ _ _ _ _ _ _ _ _ _       O
```

ABS(X)

Let us consider finally the ABS library function. This function automatically evaluates the argument, which must be in real mode, and finds its absolute value by making it positive. This may appear pointless, but it has many uses.

Thus if $A = $ ABS $(10 - X)$, then $A = 3$, when $X = 7$

$$A = 0, \text{ when } X = 10$$

$$A = 3, \text{ when } X = 17$$

and so on.

When used in conjunction with an IF statement, it gives the IF statement more flexibility.

Suppose it were required to select and print all ages in the range 21 ± 5 years from a set of ages read from data cards and print only those falling in this range. The single IF statement shown below would make this choice:

```
        IF (ABS (AGE - 21.0) - 5.0) 10, 10, 20
```

That is, if the difference between AGE and 21·0 were greater than 5, the next statement to be executed would be statement 20; otherwise statement 10, the WRITE statement for printing the ages, would be executed.

Example 3

Consider now a program which is required to sum the terms of the infinite series:

$$1 + \tfrac{1}{2} + \tfrac{1}{3} + \tfrac{1}{4} + \ldots$$

until the difference between consecutive terms becomes less than 0·001. When this condition is met the sum is to be printed out.

Flowchart for program:

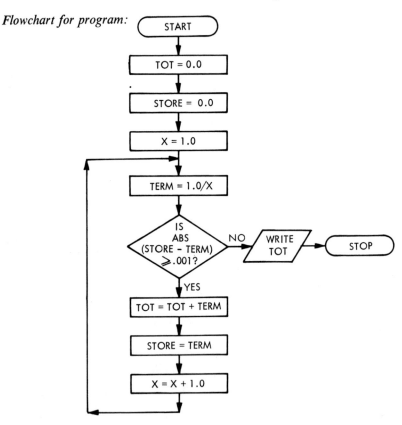

Coding for program:

```
// JOB T
// FOR
*LIST SOURCE PROGRAM
*IOCS(CARD, 1132 PRINTER)
C     PROGRAM TO ILLUSTRATE THE USE OF
C     THE ABS LIBRARY FUNCTION
      TOT = 0.0
      STORE = 0.0
      X = 1.0
```

```
  5 TERM = 1.0/X
    IF (ABS(STORE - TERM) - .001) 10, 20, 20
 20 TOT = TOT + TERM
    STORE = TERM
    X = X + 1.0
    GO TO 5
 10 WRITE (3, 30) TOT
 30 FORMAT (10X, 'TOTAL IS', F10.3)
    CALL EXIT
    END
// XEQ
```

Printer output:

```
    TOTAL IS    4.058
```

Note

(1) The variable STORE is used to store the previous term. Initially it is set equal to zero.

(2) The variable TERM evaluates the current term of the series, while TOT accumulates the sum of the series.

(3) The IF statement checks for a difference between STORE and TERM of less than 0·001. If found, a jump is made to statement 10 and the answer printed out. If not, the program continues on round the loop.

Assignment 6

(1) Using the formula given below, write a program which tabulates the time (in seconds) taken for a body, falling freely under gravity, to travel 10, 20, 30, . . ., 200 m.

$$\text{Time} = \sqrt{\frac{2 \times \text{distance}}{g}}, \text{ where } g \text{ is } 9\cdot81 \text{ metres/second/second}$$

(2) Incorporate changes into the program for (1) to place a suitable heading above the output table, which should be 'boxed' this time.

(3) There is no library function for TAN(X), but you can use the relationship:

$$\text{TANX} = \frac{\text{SIN}(X)}{\text{COS}(X)}$$

Write a program to produce a table of values for X, SIN(X), COS(X) and TANX, starting with a value of 0° and increasing by units of 5° until it terminates at 90°.

(Remember that X will first have to be converted to radians.)

(4) Given below is a function of y:

$$y = 1 + x + \frac{x^2}{2!} + \frac{x^3}{3!} + \cos(x)$$

Tabulate the values of y for values of x, starting $x = 0.00$, 0.05, 0.10, 0.15, . . ., 1.00.

Print appropriate headings above your output.

(5) A quadratic equation is one with the general form of $ax^2 + bx + c = 0$. The solution to such an equation is given by the expression:

$$x = \frac{-b \pm \sqrt{b^2 - 4ac}}{2a}$$

Write a program to do the following: read from a data card the values of a, b and c; check whether $(b^2 - 4ac)$ is positive or zero; if so, calculate and print out the results, together with the input values; if negative, print out the message 'imaginary values'. Supply 6 data cards.

(6) The Sine rule used in the solution of triangles states that:

$$\frac{a}{\sin A} = \frac{b}{\sin B} = \frac{c}{\sin C}$$

where a, b and c are the lengths of the sides of a triangle and A, B and C are the angles opposite those sides.

Write a program which will: read from a data card two angles A and B and the length of a side a; calculate the third angle C and determine the length of side c; print out the results, together with the input values, and fully label all information. A suitable title to your output might be 'Solution of Triangles—The Sine Rule'.

(7) A formula for calculating the area of any triangle, given only the lengths of three sides, is given below:

$$\text{Area} = \sqrt{s(s - a)(s - b)(s - c)}$$

where $s =$ half the sum of the sides of the triangle, i.e. $\dfrac{a + b + c}{2}$.

a, b and c are the lengths of the sides of the triangle.

Given a set of data cards, each of which contains the lengths of the three sides of a triangle, write a program to calculate and print the area of each triangle, together with the lengths of its sides.

(8) Write a program to sum the following series to the fourth decimal place:

$$\frac{1}{2!} + \frac{2}{3!} + \frac{3}{4!} + \cdots$$

Practical Session 7
The DO-Loop

In the three previous Practical Sessions we have taken a great deal of care in tabulating lists of conversion quantities, pounds and dollars, Centigrade and Fahrenheit degrees, and so on. In such cases we have to observe three important requirements:

(a) Initialise the quantity which is being converted.

(b) Increment this quantity each time the loop is executed.

(c) Test after each increment that we have not exceeded an agreed upper limit.

This Practical Session deals with a new instruction which will automatically cope with all three of the above requirements. This instruction is called the DO instruction. It is always involved in looping, that is, doing the same set of instructions over and over again, and is usually referred to by the title DO-loop.

The DO instruction is of the form shown below:

```
DO n I = MIN, MAX, INC
```

n   is always the statement number of the last instruction of the loop.

I   is called the index value of the loop and must always be an integer variable.

MIN   is either an integer constant (e.g. 1, 6, 9) or an integer variable and is the first value that the index will become, i.e. the index I is initialised to this value.

MAX   obeys exactly the same rules as MIN, but in this case it is the last or final value that I is given, i.e. MAX is the terminal value of the index.

INC   once again can be an integer constant or an integer variable. This value is the amount by which the index will increase at the beginning of every new pass through the loop.

The example below will help to clarify the various points mentioned:

```
DO 12 I = 1, 10, 2
```

The above example of a DO statement defines the range of the loop. It is to include all statements that follow the DO statement, inclusive of the last statement, statement number 12.

The index of this loop is *I*, and during the first pass through the loop *I* will have a value of 1. When all the statements of the loop have been executed, the last of which is statement 12, the computer will automatically return to the DO statement, whereupon *I* will now be assigned the new value of $1 + 2$, that is, 3. (The minimum value of *I* has now been increased automatically by the incremental value.)

When the computer returns to the beginning of the loop *I* will have a value of $3 + 2$, that is, 5, and so on, During the final pass through the loop, the index *I* will have a value of 9. This time, on reaching statement number 12, the computer will not return to the beginning of the loop but simply carry on in sequence with the statement following statement 12. In other words the looping is automatically terminated.

The CONTINUE Statement

Before going on to consider some practical examples of DO-loops, let us look at one final point which will relieve us of having to remember lots of restrictions about the last statement of a DO loop. For example, the last statement may not be a GO TO, IF, STOP, another DO statement, and so on.

We generally use a CONTINUE statement to end all DO-loops. The CONTINUE statement is a dummy statement, and the computer will treat it as a legal statement but simply do nothing when it is executed. It thus behaves as a buffer statement between statements. By using a CONTINUE statement as the last statement in a DO-loop, we can avoid the many pitfalls associated with the last statement of a DO-loop.

Here is an example of a DO-loop with a CONTINUE statement:

```
DO 12 I = 2, 20, 3
    ,,
    ,,
    other statements in the loop
    ,,
    ,,
12 CONTINUE
```

Range of the DO-loop

Example 1

To illustrate the use of the DO-loop, let us re-examine the problem given in Assignment 4, question (1). This problem in programming requires that we process *six* data cards and no more. Each data card has to contain four real numbers and we are required to find their mean and print out the answer, together with the input values.

The previous method by which we determined when six data cards had been processed was to count the number of data cards read into the computer and test this count by using an IF statement. This time a DO-loop will be used to keep track of the number of data cards read.

Flowchart for the program:

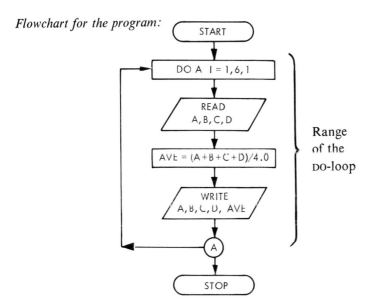

Range of the DO-loop

Note

(1) There is no IF statement and no counting system to keep check of the number of cards read. All of this is done automatically by the DO statement.

(2) The value of *I*, the index, is never actually used in the loop shown above. It merely increments by one each time the loop is commenced until it completes its sixth circuit of the loop. On completion of the sixth time round the loop, it will not return to the beginning of the loop but carry on to execute the STOP instruction.

Coding for program:

```
// JOB T
// FOR
*LIST SOURCE PROGRAM
*IOCS(CARD, 1132 PRINTER)
C      PROGRAM USING A DO-LOOP TO CONTROL
C      THE READING OF DATA CARDS
       DO 30 I = 1,6,1
       READ (2,10) A,B,C,D
10 FORMAT (4F10.2)
       AVE = (A + B + C + D)/4.
```

(Continued overleaf . . .)

```
            WRITE (3,20) A,B,C,D,AVE
        20 FORMAT (10X, 'THE AVERAGE OF', F10.2, ' ',
                          F10.2, ' ', F10.2, ' ',
          1F10.2, ' IS; F10.2)
        30 CONTINUE
           CALL EXIT
           END
    // XEQ
            2.10      32.40       6.50        .10
          316.20      21.40       6.50      10.01
           33.04      64.78      15.04      99.00
          433.10       9.20      65.10      94.33
          615.33      22.11       6.10       7.77
            9.60       3.11       4.20      10.15
          331.20      40.88     913.71      64.55
          373.10      91.60       1.00       2.56
          699.10      22.44      50.05      63.63
           71.01      36.11     917.20       3.50
```

Printer output:

```
THE AVERAGE OF    2.10 32.40    6.50    .10 IS    10.27
THE AVERAGE OF 316.20 21.40    6.50 10.01 IS    88.52
THE AVERAGE OF   33.04 64.78  15.04 99.00 IS    52.96
THE AVERAGE OF 433.10  9.20  65.10 94.33 IS  150.43
THE AVERAGE OF 615.33 22.11    6.10   7.77 IS  162.82
THE AVERAGE OF    9.60  3.11    4.20 10.15 IS     6.76
```

Example 2

In Example 1 the actual value of the index *I* was never used in the loop. The following program demonstrates the use of the current value of the index. But, note, we are never at any time allowed to place the index variable on the left-hand side of an equals sign. In other words, the value of the index in a DO-loop must never be changed, except by the normal incrementing action of the DO-loop itself.

Consider the following problem and its solution. For the sake of comparison, two programs are shown. One uses a DO-loop, the other does not.

A cuboid starts off as a unit cube of side 1 cm and at each stage in its expansion, its length (*L*) increases by 1 cm. It is required to write a program to compute its surface area (SA) and its volume (VOL) at each stage of expansion.

82

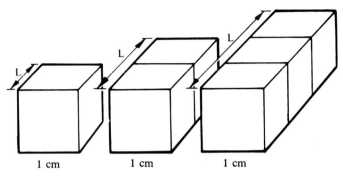

1 cm   1 cm   1 cm

Because only the length of the cuboid increases at each expansion while the end face remains 1 cm square, the formulae for finding the surface area and the volume reduce to:

$$\text{SA} = 4L + 2$$
$$\text{VOL} = L$$

Flowchart for program 1:   *Flowchart for program* 2:

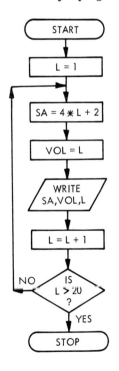

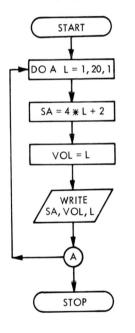

Coding for program 1:

```
// JOB T
// FOR
*LIST SOURCE PROGRAM
*IOCS(CARD, 1132 PRINTER)
C       PROGRAM ON THE EXPANDING CUBOID -
C       WITHOUT THE USE OF A DO-LOOP
        L = 1
      6 SA = 4*L + 2
        VOL = L
        WRITE (3,20) SA, VOL, L
     20 FORMAT (10X,'THE SURFACE AREA IS', F10.0,
                         2X, 'THE VOLUME IS', F10.0,
        12X, 'WHEN THE LENGTH IS', I6)
        L = L + 1
        IF (20 - L) 12,6,6
     12 CALL EXIT
        END
// XEQ
```

Coding for program 2:

```
// JOB T
// FOR
*LIST SOURCE PROGRAM
*IOCS(CARD, 1132 PRINTER)
C       PROGRAM ON THE EXPANDING CUBOID -
C       WITH THE USE OF A DO-LOOP
        DO 300 L = 1, 20, 1
        SA = 4*L + 2
        VOL = L
        WRITE (3,20) SA, VOL, L
     20 FORMAT (10X,'THE SURFACE AREA IS', F10.0,
                         2X, 'THE VOLUME IS', F10.0,
        12X, 'WHEN THE LENGTH IS', I6)
    300 CONTINUE
        CALL EXIT
        END
// XEQ
```

In program 2 the current value of the index L was continually being used during each pass through the loop, but more important the value of L was not changed by any arithmetic statement in the loop.

Note

(1) The minimum value of any index must be 1.

(2) The incremental value cannot be zero or fractional.

(3) If the incremental value of a DO statement is not actually stated, then it is assumed by the computer to be 1. In other words, if the

84

incremental value of a DO-loop is 1, then only the MIN and MAX values need be stated.

(4) The MAX value should always be greater than the MIN value.

Printer output (identical for each program):

```
THE SURFACE AREA IS   6    THE VOLUME IS    1
                           WHEN THE LENGTH IS    1
THE SURFACE AREA IS  10    THE VOLUME IS    2
                           WHEN THE LENGTH IS    2
THE SURFACE AREA IS  14    THE VOLUME IS    3
                           WHEN THE LENGTH IS    3

            . . . and so on, up to:

THE SURFACE AREA IS  74    THE VOLUME IS   18
                           WHEN THE LENGTH IS  18
THE SURFACE AREA IS  78    THE VOLUME IS   19
                           WHEN THE LENGTH IS  19
THE SURFACE AREA IS  82    THE VOLUME IS   20
                           WHEN THE LENGTH IS  20
```

Example 3

Let us now consider a program which uses an incremental value other than unity. A program is required to produce the sum of all the odd numbers between 100 and 200.

Flowchart for program:

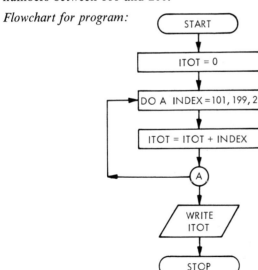

85

Coding for program:

```
// JOB T
// FOR
*LIST SOURCE PROGRAM
*IOCS(CARD, 1132 PRINTER)
C      PROGRAM TO DEMONSTRATE DO-LOOP USAGE
C      WITH AN INCREMENT GREATER THAN 1
       ITOT = 0.0
       DO 96 INDEX = 101,199,2
       ITOT = ITOT + INDEX
   96 CONTINUE
       WRITE (3,40) ITOT
   40 FORMAT (20X, 'THE TOTAL OF THE ODD NUMBERS
                    BETWEEN 100 AND 200 IS', I6)
       CALL EXIT
       END
// XEQ
```

Printer output:

THE TOTAL OF THE ODD NUMBERS BETWEEN 100 AND 200
                                              IS 7500

Assignment 7

(1) Write a program using a DO-loop to sum the first fifty even numbers in the set of natural numbers. Your output should take the form of a running total.

(2) Write a program to make use of a DO-loop to produce a conversion table of miles to kilometres. Your table should range from 1 to 20 miles. (*Caution*: Do not use integer mode in your arithmetic statement for this program.)

(3) Write a program to calculate simple interest, given a set of data cards (not more than six) each containing the principal, rate and time. Control the reading of the cards by using a DO-loop. Input values as well as results are required in a fully labelled, tabulated and boxed output.

(4) Write a program to evaluate the function $f(x)$ defined below:

$$f(x) = ax^2 + bx + c \qquad 0 \leqslant x \leqslant 20$$

The values of a, b and c are to be read from data cards. Make use of one DO-loop to increment x from 0 to 20 by steps of 1, and at each new increment of x print out the input values of a, b and c, together with the value of x and $f(x)$. (That is, for each data card containing an a, b and c, there will be twenty printed results.)

86

(5) Using a DO-loop, evaluate the series given below to ten terms. (Take two terms at a time in summing this series.)

$$4(1 - \tfrac{1}{3} + \tfrac{1}{5} - \tfrac{1}{7} + \tfrac{1}{9} - \ldots)$$

(6) The stopping distance of a car travelling at V km/hr, when the brakes are then applied, is given by the expression:

$$D = \frac{88}{1875} V^2$$

where D is the distance in metres and V is the initial speed in km/hr.
Write a program to produce by means of a DO-loop a table of the stopping distances for the range of speeds from 10 km/hr to 100 km/hr in increments of 5 km/hr.

(7) Write a program to produce a tabulated output of the factorials of all the natural numbers in the range 1 to 10 inclusive.

(8) Using a DO-loop, write a program to produce a 29 times multiplication table. Annotate your output.

Practical Session 8
Arrays

In Practical Session 7 we discovered that DO-loops are useful because they can be used to accomplish three things at once. They can initialise the index of the loop, increment it, and finally terminate it once the index has reached the maximum limit specified in the DO statement.

In this Practical Session we are going to examine how DO-loops can be used to control computer operations involving lists, or *arrays* as they are called in computer terminology. Lists are very familiar to us in their various forms, lists of telephone numbers, prices, examination marks, football scores, and so on.

DIMENSION Statement

Because lists, or arrays can be very large and the memory size of a computer is limited, it is necessary to give the computer advance warning of the maximum number of items that the array will contain. By so doing, the computer will be able to reserve the necessary space in its memory. We provide the computer with this information by using the DIMENSION statement.

As an example, let us assume that we have an array called LIST, and we decide that it will not contain more than forty items, or more correctly *elements*. Then the required DIMENSION statement will be:

```
DIMENSION LIST (40)
```

The word DIMENSION begins in card column 7, as do most other Fortran statements. If there were more than one array to be used in our program, then we would simply add their names and maximum sizes to the DIMENSION statement, separating the array specifications by means of a comma. Suppose that the arrays N, AGE and MARK are required in a program, and they have the maximum specifications 10, 30 and 60 respectively. The DIMENSION statement will be:

```
DIMENSION  N(10), AGE(30), MARK(60)
```

Note

(1) Array names obey the same naming rules as for other variables.

(2) All DIMENSION statements are placed at the beginning of the program.

Reading in an Array

Let us now study a problem concerning the array of marks for an English examination for a class of twenty pupils. The problem is how do we get this list of marks into the computer? One way might be to continue as we have done in the past and find a new variable name for each of the twenty English marks. Thus, to read this data into the computer, our READ statement might appear something like this:

```
READ (2,10) ENG1, ENG2, ENG3, ...., , ENG20
```

This is cumbersome, especially if we are performing a computer-size problem such as processing the English marks for the City of Glasgow or the whole of Scotland. But there is an easier way, and this has been built into the Fortran system. We can use a *subscript*. In ordinary mathematics it might appear as, say a_1, but in Fortran it must appear as $A(1)$. That is, the subscript must be enclosed in brackets. In the example just cited A would be the name of the array.

Using this technique, our twenty English marks will be stored by the twenty individual variables, ENG(1), ENG(2), ENG(3), , ENG(20). This has two major advantages. The first is that we do not have to think up twenty different names. The second is that we can locate any individual examination mark from the list of twenty merely by specifying the correct subscript to the array name. This means that if we wished to print, say, the examination mark for pupil number 20 in the register, we would write the following instruction:

```
      WRITE (3,60) ENG(20)
60 FORMAT (1X, F10.2)
```

To read the list of twenty examination marks from a data card into the computer, we would write the instruction:

```
      READ (2,40) (ENG (I), I = 1,20)
40 FORMAT (20F3.1)
```

Notice that the READ list is somewhat different from any that you have met before. The array and its associated specifications are all enclosed within a bracket. The array is given a general subscript I, say (it must be an integer variable). Next to it, but separated from it by a comma, is something which you may recognise from a DO statement, an index which starts with a value of 1 and finished with a value of 20.

When the READ statement is performed, the computer will read the data card which will, of course, contain all twenty examination marks. The first examination mark will be read into array element ENG(1), the second into ENG(2), and third into ENG(3), and so on, until all the array elements, including ENG(20), have been satisfied. It is important to appreciate two points here:

(a) The index I automatically increments by one each time a mark is read in. This is sometimes known as 'implied DO-looping'.

(b) The FORMAT statement has accounted for all twenty marks.

Writing out an Array

The procedure for writing out all twenty marks is much the same as for reading them in. To write them out, we would simply write:

```
    WRITE (3,50) (ENG (I), I = 1,20)
50 FORMAT (10X, 20F5.1)
```

These statements would automatically write out all twenty English marks.

We can, of course, read-in and write-out more than one array. It is merely added to the READ or WRITE list and separated from its neighbour by a comma.

Example 1

Consider a program to read in the twenty English marks in the problem considered above, add them up, average them, and write out the input array, together with its total and average.

Flowchart for program:

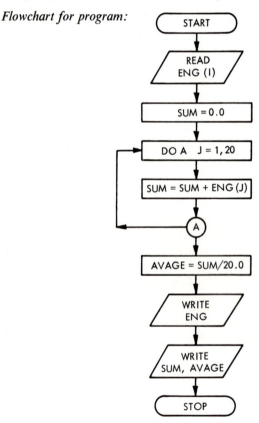

Coding for program:

```
// JOB T
// FOR
*LIST SOURCE PROGRAM
*IOCS(CARD, 1132 PRINTER)
C      THIS PROGRAM IS AN EXERCISE IN READING
C      INTO THE COMPUTER AN ARRAY AND THEN
C      WRITING IT OUT AGAIN
       DIMENSION ENG(20)
       READ (2,20) (ENG(I), I = 1,20)
    20 FORMAT (20F3.1)
       SUM = 0.0
       DO 100 J = 1,20
       SUM = SUM + ENG(J)
   100 CONTINUE
       AVAGE = SUM/20.0
       WRITE (3,30) (ENG(J), J = 1,20)
    30 FORMAT (10X, 20F5.1)
       WRITE (3,40) SUM, AVAGE
    40 FORMAT (30X, 'SUM =', F6.1, 5X, 'AVERAGE =',
                                          F6.1)
       CALL EXIT
       END
// XEQ
6153246179123162576668728337597434996137248319621 0
                                           1515669363
```

(*Note:* The data card need not necessarily contain decimal points, see Appendix B.)

Printer output:

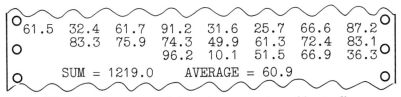

```
61.5   32.4   61.7   91.2   31.6   25.7   66.6   87.2
       83.3   75.9   74.3   49.9   61.3   72.4   83.1
              96.2   10.1   51.5   66.9   36.3
       SUM = 1219.0      AVERAGE = 60.9
```

(*The first three lines of the printer output would actually print out in a single line, with* SUM *and* AVERAGE *on a second line.*)

Finding the Largest Element in an Array

We have seen that lists of data can be read into a computer and that this data can be acted upon by DO-loop and arrays. The combination of DO-loops and arrays provides us with a most useful and flexible method of dealing with data inside the computer.

91

Suppose that we wish to select the largest element in an array. The method employed is essentially a comparison technique. The first element of the array is taken to be the largest, regardless of whether it is or not. It is placed into the variable BIG. Every other element of the array is then compared with BIG. As soon as an element is found which is bigger than that in BIG, it is immediately stored in BIG, overwriting the previous value. When the last element of the array has been thus processed, the variable BIG should contain the highest mark in the test.

Example 2

Let us consider a program that will select the highest mark in the English examination which we considered in Example 1, and print out not only the mark, but also its position in the array and the entire array itself, so that we can visually check the results.

Coding for program:

```
// JOB T
// FOR
*LIST SOURCE PROGRAM
*IOCS(CARD, 1132 PRINTER)
C      PROGRAM TO DEMONSTRATE THE VERSATILITY
C      OF ARRAYS AND DO-LOOPS
       DIMENSION ENG(100)
       READ (2,10)N
    10 FORMAT (I6)
       READ (2,20) (ENG(I), I = 1,N)
    20 FORMAT (20F3.1)
       BIG = ENG(1)
       DO 100 I = 2,N
       IF (BIG - ENG(I)) 50, 100, 100
    50 BIG = ENG(I)
       IPOSN = I
   100 CONTINUE
       WRITE (3,60) (ENG(I), I = 1,N)
    60 FORMAT (2X, 'THE INPUT ARRAY IS',20F5.1)
       WRITE (3,70) BIG, IPOSN
    70 FORMAT (2X, 'THE HIGHEST MARK IS', 'F6.1,
                    6X, 'ITS POSITION IS', I6)
       CALL EXIT
       END
// XEQ
    10
6153246179123162576668728337 59
```

Flowchart for program:

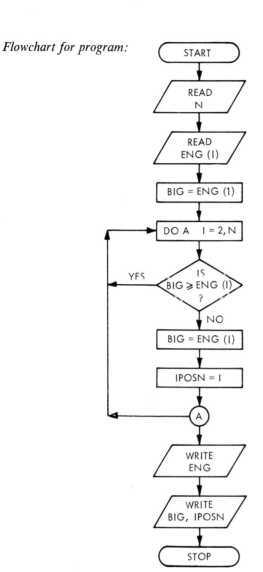

START

READ
N

READ
ENG (I)

BIG = ENG (1)

DO A   I = 2, N

IS
BIG ⩾ ENG (I)
?

YES

NO

BIG = ENG (I)

IPOSN = I

A

WRITE
ENG

WRITE
BIG, IPOSN

STOP

Printer output:

```
THE INPUT ARRAY IS  61.5   32.4   61.7   91.2   31.6
                    25.7   66.6   87.2   83.3   75.9
THE HIGHEST MARK IS 91.2            ITS POSITION IS   4
```

*(The input array above would be in one complete line of
output when printed.)*

93

Note

(1) The DIMENSION statement is necessary because the program uses an array.

(2) The extra READ instruction for reading in the value of N, the size of the array, is included to make the program general. If N were fixed at 5, say, the program would only be useful in dealing with 5 element arrays. As it stands, the program will cope with any size of array up to a maximum of 100 elements. It is the DIMENSION statement which determines the maximum. Thus, we can read in any integer value for N punched on a data card less than or equal to 100.

(3) The DO statement starts at element number 2 since we have assumed that element 1 is the largest element of the array.

(4) The IF statement checks each element of the array against that stored in BIG. As soon as it finds one that is greater than BIG, statement 50 replaces the current value of BIG by the new one. The value of I (the position in the array) is then stored in IPOSN, and the search continues.

(5) The technique shown above is the basis of many more complicated programs involving searching.

Example 3

Let us now study how an array can be used to assist in the evaluation of a polynomial. Write a program which will read eight values of a and only one of x and compute the value of the function $f(x)$ as defined below:

$$f(x) = a_1 + a_2 x + a_3 x^2 + a_4 x^3 + a_5 x^4 + a_6 x^5 + a_7 x^6 + a_8 x^7$$

Coding for program:

```
// JOB T
// FOR
*LIST SOURCE PROGRAM
*IOCS(CARD, 1132 PRINTER)
C     PROGRAM TO DEMONSTRATE THE USE OF AN
C     ARRAY IN POLYNOMIAL EVALUATION
      DIMENSION COEFF(8)
    1 READ (2,10)X, (COEFF(I), I = 1,8)
   10 FORMAT (9F6.1)
      IF (X - 9999.0) 12, 99, 12
```

```
 12 SUM = COEFF(1)
    DO 100 L = 2,8
    TERM = COEFF(L)*X**(L-1)
    SUM = SUM + TERM
100 CONTINUE
    WRITE (3,20) SUM
 20 FORMAT (10X,'THE VALUE OF THIS FUNCTION IS',
                                           F10.1)
    GO TO 1
 99 CALL EXIT
    END
// XEQ
    1.0   3.0   6.1   5.4   3.5   10.4   1.5   7.4   1.0
    3.5   1.6   2.7   4.3   9.1    8.6   2.1   1.0   0.7
    9999.0
```

Flowchart for program:

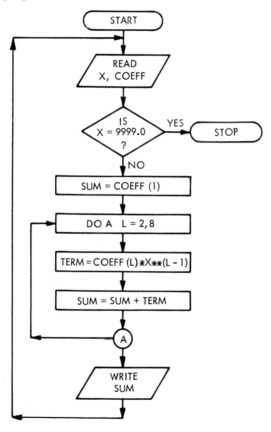

Printer output:

```
  THE VALUE OF THIS FUNCTION IS 38.2
  THE VALUE OF THIS FUNCTION IS 9189.4
```

Note

(1) The last card technique has been used in this program to keep it general.

(2) The DO-loop starts with an index of 2, since the first term of the polynomial has already been added to the sum.

(3) The two arithmetic statements contained within the DO-loop can, of course, be incorporated in a single statement.

Assignment 8

(1) Write a program to read an array of real numbers, find the smallest element of the array, and print it out, together with the original array so that it can be checked visually. Adjust the size of the array so that all the required data values for it can be accommodated on one data card.

(2) Write a program to read into the computer the array you used in question (1) again, but this time extend your program to pick out not only the smallest element but also the largest element. Arrange to print out the entire array on one line of printer output, and on a second line print the largest and smallest elements of the array, together with their positional values in the array, i.e. their subscripts.

(3) Write a program that will utilise two arrays, the first to store the original array and the second to store the elements of the original array but in the reverse order. That is, you program should store the first element of the input array in the last element of the other array; the second element of the input array in the last but one element of the other array; and so on until the entire input array has been processed. Print out both arrays, fully labelled, one on each line of printer output.

(4) Write a program to read an array and then proceed to add all the odd subscripted elements and all the even subscripted elements separately. Print out the array and both totals, fully labelled.

(5) Without reading in any data, write a program which will place the squares of the first eight natural numbers into an array called SQARS and the cubes of the same set of natural numbers into an array called CUBES. Each of the elements of the array called SQARS should then be subtracted from its corresponding element in the array called CUBES and the result placed in an array called DIFFS. Print out each of the three arrays, fully labelled, on a different line of output.

(6) Read into the computer an array of 50 single-digit numbers from a single data card. Write your program so that it will check each element of this array and print out the number of elements which have a value of 5 or greater. Print out also the original array on another output line.

(7) Write a program to read an array of coefficients and a value of y so that it will evaluate the function:

$$f(y) = a_1 y^8 + a_2 y^7 + a_3 y^6 + a_4 y^5 + a_5 y^4 + a_6 y^3 + a_7 y^2 + a_8 y + a_9$$

Design your program to evaluate six different sets of data and fully label all outputs.

(8) Below is shown a sample data card showing bank number, principal, rate, and time in years, in that order:

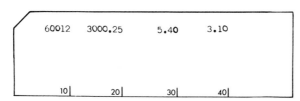

Develop a program to process four of these data cards and calculate the simple interest in each case. It is important that your program should be written so that it will print out only the four answers after *all* four data cards have been processed. (*Hint:* Make use of arrays to store your answers while you are processing the new data.)

Practical Session 9
Two-Dimensional Arrays

We saw in Practical Session 8 that the use of arrays introduces a new flexibility into programming, making it possible to store and manipulate large quantities of data, for example, choosing the largest or smallest value from a long list. This Practical Session will also deal with arrays, but will go one stage further and look at *two-dimensional* arrays. This type of array is probably more familiar to you in the form of *matrices* or *determinants*, e.g.

$$\begin{pmatrix} 2 & 6 \\ 5 & 4 \end{pmatrix} \qquad \begin{pmatrix} 2 & 6 & 4 & 8 \\ 5 & 3 & 7 & 1 \\ 4 & 1 & 9 & 6 \end{pmatrix}$$

$$(1) \qquad\qquad\qquad (2)$$

Matrix (1) is said to be a 2 by 2 array (giving the *row* dimension first, and then the *column* dimension). Matrix (2) is a 3 by 4 array. Such arrays extend over two dimensions, to form a table rather than a single dimension array forming a simple list. Another form of two-dimensional array would be a table of, say, prices of various items against their quality:

	Quality 1	Quality 2	Quality 3
Item 1	16	18	22
Item 2	36	40	48
Item 3	1	2	4

Nested DO-loops

Up to this point programs have involved the use of only a single DO-loop. But we can also use a DO-loop within an existing DO-loop. This structure of DO-loops contained within DO-loops is called *nesting*. Programming which involves two-dimensional arrays inevitably involves such nested DO-loops. The maximum number of *nests* is 25. When a DO-loop is nested within another DO-loop, the inner loop is cycled to completion for each and every cycle of the outer loop.

Certain forms of nesting are legal, while other forms are illegal. The diagrams shown below specify both of these types:

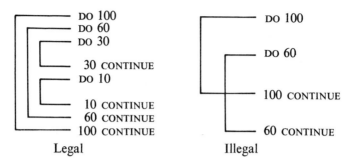

Legal	Illegal

A final important point concerning DO-loops is that you must never cause a branch into the loop itself, thus avoiding the DO statement. If this were allowed to happen, the index of the loop would not have been defined for that loop.

Example 1
In the light of these facts on nesting, let us now look at an example. A program is required to compute and print out a table of addition facts in the following manner:

```
 2 =  1 +  1
 3 =  2 +  1
 4 =  3 +  1
 -    -    -
 -    -    -
10 =  9 +  1
 3 =  1 +  2
 4 =  2 +  2
 5 =  3 +  2
 -    -    -
 -    -    -
20 = 10 + 10
```

We shall demonstrate two methods for obtaining the above output. One uses nested DO-loops, the other does not. We shall call the program that does not use nested DO-loops program 1, and the program that does use them program 2. The flowchart and coding for each program are shown overleaf.

Flowchart for program 1:   *Flowchart for program* 2:

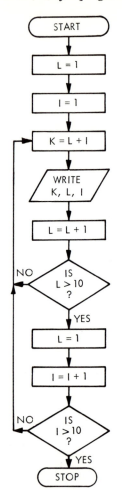
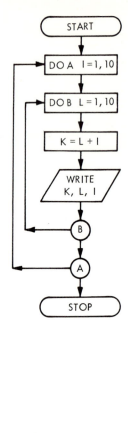

Coding for program 1:

```
// JOB T
// FOR
*LIST SOURCE PROGRAM
*IOCS(CARD, 1132 PRINTER)
C      PROGRAM TO PRINT ADDITION FACTS WITHOUT
C      THE AID OF DO-LOOPS
       L = 1
       I = 1
    99 K = L + I
       WRITE (3,10) K,L,I
```

```
  10 FORMAT (20X, I4, ' = ', I4, ' + ', I4)
     L = L + 1
     IF (10-L) 66,99,99
  66 L = 1
     I = I + 1
     IF (10-I) 33,99,99
  33 CALL EXIT
     END
// XEQ
```

Coding for program 2:

```
// JOB T
// FOR
*LIST SOURCE PROGRAM
*IOCS(CARD, 1132 PRINTER)
C      PROGRAM TO PRINT ADDITION FACTS USING
C      NESTED DO-LOOPS
       DO 100 I = 1,10
       DO 200 L = 1,10
       K = L + I
       WRITE (3,10) K,L,I
  10 FORMAT (20X, I4, ' = ', I4, ' + ', I4)
 200 CONTINUE
 100 CONTINUE
     CALL EXIT
     END
// XEQ
```

Both programs will produce the desired printer output shown on
page 99.

Note

(1) There is a distinct cycling effect in program 2. The inner loop, i.e.
index L, is cycling ten times for each cycle of the outer loop, index I.

(2) One loop is completely enclosed by the other—there is no overlap.
It is noteworthy that one is allowed to end inner and outer loops on
the same CONTINUE statement.

(3) It is much more efficient programming to use nested DO-loops in
the above program.

Example 2

Let us now consider an example which utilises nested DO-loops in
conjunction with arrays. The problem is to arrange a set of ten numbers
in descending numerical order.

To illustrate the principle used in the programming of such a problem,
consider arranging the four array elements $A(1)$, $A(2)$, $A(3)$, $A(4)$, into

101

descending order. The first stage is to compare each element in turn with $A(1)$ and as soon as an element which is larger in content is encountered, interchange the contents of both. At the completion of this stage $A(1)$ will contain the largest value of all the elements. The second stage is to compare each of the remaining elements with $A(2)$ in a similar way. At the end of this stage $A(2)$ will contain the second largest value. This process is continued until the last element automatically contains the smallest value. (See diagram below.)

Stage 1	$A(1)$	$A(2)$	$A(3)$	$A(4)$
Stage 2	$A(1)$	$A(2)$	$A(3)$	$A(4)$
Stage 3	$A(1)$	$A(2)$	$A(3)$	$A(4)$

A practical example starting with the numbers 6·0, 1·0, 7·0, 4·0 would go through the following interchanges:

Stage 1	7·0	1·0	6·0	4·0
Stage 2	7·0	6·0	1·0	4·0
Stage 3	7·0	6·0	4·0	1·0

Putting this into the language of Fortran:

```
      DO 100 I = 2,4
      DO 100 J = I,4
      IF (A(I-1) - A(J)) 66,100,100
   66 STORE = A(J)
      A(J) = A(I-1)
      A(I-1) = STORE
  100 CONTINUE
```

Note

(1) It is allowable to have a subscript of the form $n \pm k$, where n is an integer variable and k is an integer constant.

(2) The outer loop controls the basic array element being compared, e.g. $A(1)$ in Stage 1, $A(2)$ in Stage 2, and so on. Each time the outer loop increments, the inner loop cycles up through the remainder of the array. For this reason, the inner loop index is set equal to the current value of I.

(3) The IF statement simply carries out the comparison. On finding that $A(J) > A(I-1)$, it goes on to an interchanging routine, otherwise it bypasses this.

(4) The actual interchange of the contents of $A(J)$ and $A(I-1)$ involves three separate instructions. If you simply had:

$$A(J) = A(I-1)$$

102

then the contents of $A(J)$ would be automatically overwritten by the contents of $A(I - 1)$. For this reason $A(J)$ is first stored in STORE and then written into $A(I - 1)$. Finally, to complete the switch, the contents of STORE are assigned to $A(I - 1)$.

Flowchart for program:

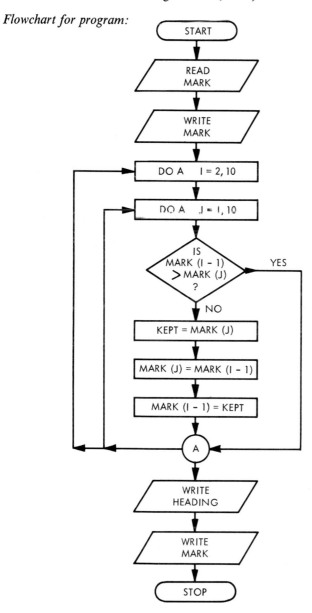

Coding for program:

```
// JOB T
// FOR
*LIST SOURCE PROGRAM
*IOCS(CARD, 1132 PRINTER)
C      PROGRAM TO SORT THE CONTENTS OF
C      AN ARRAY INTO DESCENDING ORDER
       DIMENSION MARK(10)
       READ (2,10) (MARK(I), I = 1,10)
    10 FORMAT (10I4)
       WRITE (3,20) (MARK(I), I = 1,10)
    20 FORMAT (10X, 'ORIGINAL ARRAY', 10I8)
       DO 100 I = 2,10
       DO 100 J = I,10
       IF (MARK(I-1) - MARK(J)) 66, 100, 100
    66 KEPT = MARK(J)
       MARK(J) = MARK(I-1)
       MARK(I-1) = KEPT
   100 CONTINUE
       WRITE (3,30)
    30 FORMAT (10X, 'THE ARRAY SORTED INTO
                           DESCENDING ORDER')
       WRITE (3,40) (MARK(I), I=1,10)
    40 FORMAT (10X, 10I8)
       CALL EXIT
       END
// XEQ
       61   54   76   41   2   94   83   3   21   14
```

Printer output:

```
ORIGINAL ARRAY 61  54  76  41   2  94  83   3  21  14
THE ARRAY SORTED INTO DESCENDING ORDER
                 94  83  76  61  54  41  21  14   3   2
```

DIMENSION Statement

We must give a DIMENSION statement in any program which involves a two-dimensional array, as we do with the one-dimension array. That is, we must state the maximum size of the intended array. For example, if we had a 4 by 3 array called LIST and a 10 by 15 array called MARK then the correct dimension statement would be:

        DIMENSION LIST(4,3), MARK(10,15)

Reading into a Two-Dimensional Array

The reading of data into a two-dimensional array is done in much the same way as for one-dimensional arrays. We make use of implied DO-loops, but in this case we require to cycle two indices because of the double dimension.

Suppose that we have to read twelve values into an array called LIST and use the data card shown below. The proper READ statement would be:

```
     READ (2,10) ((LIST(I,J),I=4),J=3)
10 FORMAT (12I4)
```

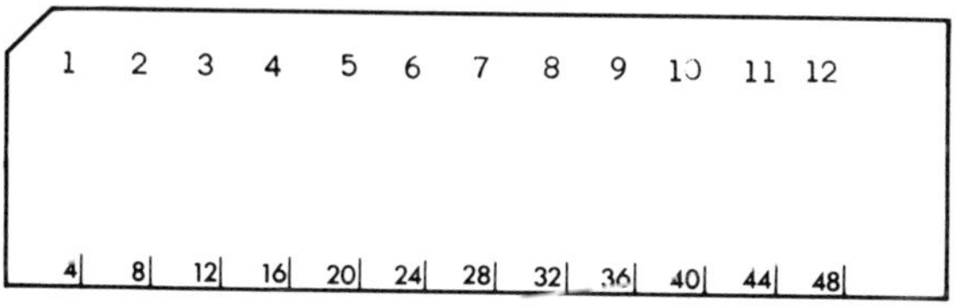

Remembering that the first subscript, I in this case, is the row and the second subscript J the column, the array would be filled in the following order:

$$
\begin{array}{ccc}
1 & 5 & 9 \\
2 & 6 & 10 \\
3 & 7 & 11 \\
4 & 8 & 12 \\
\end{array}
$$

If the READ statement had been:

```
     READ (2,10) ((LIST(I,J), J=3), I=4)
```

the array would have been filled in a different order:

$$
\begin{array}{ccc}
1 & 2 & 3 \\
4 & 5 & 6 \\
7 & 8 & 9 \\
10 & 11 & 12 \\
\end{array}
$$

Thus, numbers can be stored in an array in any way we choose, depending solely on which subscript is first cycled.

Generally, if a data card is punched with the numbers so sequenced that they are to be read into the array, A say, in rows, the READ statement would be:

```
     READ (2,10) ((A(I,J),J=1,N), I=1,M)
```

If the data card had this data sequenced in columns, then the appropriate READ statement would be:

```
     READ (2,10) ((A(I,J),I=1,M),J=1,N)
```

Printing out a Two-Dimensional Array

The printing out of a two-dimensional array is much the same as the reading in. It is usual to print an entire row at a time. An appropriate WRITE statement for our array called LIST would be:

```
    WRITE(2,20) ((LIST(I,J),J=1,3),I=1,4)
 20 FORMAT (10X, 3I8/10X, 3I8/10X, 3I8/10X, 3I8)
```

Note the / character appearing in the FORMAT statement. A / (*slash*) used in this fashion within a FORMAT statement instructs the computer to jump to a new line. Having printed out three values in the first line of print of array LIST, it jumps to a new line and, leaving 10 blank spaces, prints out another three values of the array, and so on until all four lines or rows of the array have been printed.

Example 3

Let us sum up the subject of two-dimensional arrays in the form of a program. The program will simply read in twelve values into a 4 by 3 array, sum all the elements row by row, and finally print out the original array and the sum total of all the elements.

Flowchart for program:

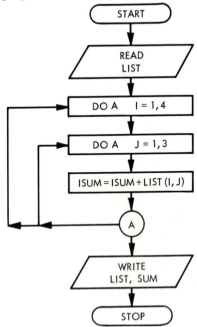

106

Coding for program:

```
// JOB T
// FOR
*LIST SOURCE PROGRAM
*IOCS(CARD, 1132 PRINTER)
C       PROGRAM TO DEMONSTRATE THE HANDLING
C       OF DOUBLE SUBSCRIPTED ARRAYS
        DIMENSION LIST (4,3)
        READ (2,20) ((LIST(I,J),J=1,3),I=1,4)
     20 FORMAT (12I4)
        ISUM = 0
        DO 100 I = 1,4
        DO 100 J = 1,3
        ISUM = ISUM + LIST (I,J)
    100 CONTINUE
        WRITE (3,30) ((LIST(I,J),J=1,3),I=1,4),ISUM
     30 FORMAT (10X,3I8/10X,3I8/10X,3I8/10X,3I8/20X,
                                   'SUM = ',I6)
        CALL EXIT
        END
// XEQ
     1  6  4  10  8  7  4  13  15  10  4  3
```

Printer output:

```
         1     6     4
        10     8     7
         4    13    15
        10     4     3
           SUM = 85
```

Note

The statement

$$ISUM = ISUM + LIST(M, N)$$

could have been used within the nested DO-loops, provided that the indices of the outer and inner loops were M and N respectively.

Example 4

Let us now look at another program, this time one involving a 4 × 4 array. It is required that all the row elements become column elements and all the column elements become row elements. Both the original and final arrays are to be printed out.

One of the simplest methods of doing this is to place each element of the original array into the appropriate elemental position in a new array and then print out both arrays.

Flowchart for program:

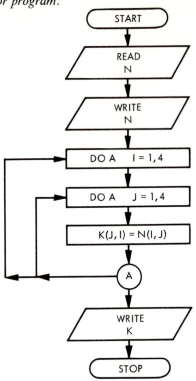

Coding for program:

```
// JOB T
// FOR
*LIST SOURCE PROGRAM
*IOCS(CARD, 1132 PRINTER)
C     PROGRAM TO DEMONSTRATE THE MANIPULATION
C     OF ARRAY ELEMENTS
      DIMENSION N(4,4), K(4,4)
      READ (2,10) ((N(I,J), J = 1,4), I =1,4)
   10 FORMAT (16I4)
      WRITE (3,20) ((N(I,J), J = 1,4), I = 1,4)
   20 FORMAT (10X, 'THE ORIGINAL ARRAY IS'/30X,
               4I8/30X, 4I8/30X, 4I8/30X, 4I8/)
      DO 66 I = 1,4
      DO 66 J = 1,4
      K(J,I) = N(I,J)
   66 CONTINUE
      WRITE (3,30) ((K(I,J), J = 1,4), I = 1,4)
```

```
      30 FORMAT (10X,'THE FINAL ARRAY IS'/30X,
                    4I8/30X, 4I8/30X, 4I8/30X, 4I8/)
         CALL EXIT
         END
// XEQ
      1 2 3 4 5 6 7 8 9 10 11 12 13 14 15 16
```

Printer output:

```
  THE ORIGINAL ARRAY IS
                    1    2    3    4
                    5    6    7    8
                    9   10   11   12
                   13   14   15   16
  THE FINAL ARRAY IS
                    1    5    9   13
                    2    6   10   14
                    3    7   11   15
                    4    8   12   16
```

Assignment 9

(1) Write a program which will read the set of numbers shown on the
data card below. Your program should arrange them into ascending
numerical order. The output should consist of the original unsorted
array and the final sorted sequence of numbers fully labelled.

6 1 7 2 9 8 5 3 0 4

(2) Construct a program to read and sum the ten numbers shown on the
data card below. These numbers are to be read into a 5 × 2 array
called *N*. Print out the array *N*, together with the sum of all the
elements of this array. Label your output.

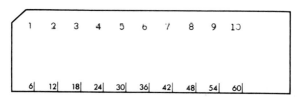

```
 1   2   3   4   5   6   7   8   9  10

 6|  12|  18|  24|  30|  36|  42|  48|  54|  60|
```

109

(3) Use the values shown in the following data card:

3 9 8 1 2 7 6 4 5 0 3 2

to fill an array called LIST, as in diagram ①. Your program should
then manipulate the array elements so that the elements of the
centre columns are interchanged as shown in diagram ②. Print
out both of these arrays fully labelled.

```
3  1  6  0        3  6  1  0
9  2  4  3        9  4  2  3
8  7  5  2        8  5  7  2
     ①                ②
```

(4) Write a program to read the same data card as in question (3),
again placing the values shown in ① above into an array called
LIST. Sum only the elements of columns 2 and 3 and print out the
array together with this sum.

(5) Read twenty-five values of your choice arranged on a single data
card into a 5 × 5 array. Your program should sum only those
elements of the array which have a value of 4 or less. Print the array
and this total.

(6) Write a program using the values shown on the card below to fill
a 4 × 4 array. The program should be designed to select both the
largest and smallest values of this array and print them out. The
output should be fully labelled and include the array.

6 9 1 2 2 1 4 8 6 8 1 7 9 2 0 1

(7) Using the data card in question (6), read the elements into the
square 4 × 4 array called IRST. Using this single array, design a
program which will interchange the values of the elements in the
way shown below. Note that the pivotal diagonal elements remain
unchanged.

(8) Read a data card containing the prices of different items of various qualities to fill the following two-dimensional array.

$$\begin{array}{ccc} 16 & 18 & 22 \\ 36 & 40 & 48 \\ 1 & 2 & 4 \end{array}$$

The first row is item 1 and the three columns, starting from the left, are the three different qualities in which the item is available, i.e. quality 1, quality 2, quality 3. Construct your program to read in data cards, a sample of which is shown below, which contains the item number, the quality and the quantity of items bought:

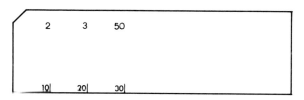

Calculate the total cost of the goods by locating the correct price from the array and print out an invoice in the following form. (Use the end card technique.)

```
INVOICE DATED 25/FEB/71
ITEM        QUALITY       QUANTITY        COST
  2            3             50           2400
  _            _             _             _
  _            _             _             _
                                        _____
                             TOTAL
```

Practical Session 10
Multi-Array Programs

Practical Session 9 demonstrated some of the ways in which programming was capable of handling two-dimensional arrays. This Practical Session will continue to describe techniques for handling this type of array but will be developed so that more than one array can appear in the same program.

Using more than One Data Card

Before considering multi-array programs, we shall look at another problem. You may have noticed that all of the examples in Practical Session 9 were restricted to the use of a single data card to hold the values of any array used in the programs. Larger arrays obviously require more data, and there comes a point, depending on the size of the array, when it is necessary to spill onto more and more data cards. Consider filling up a 3 by 4 array called MARK with twelve data values spread over two cards instead of one, as shown below:

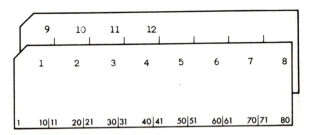

The two data cards have to be read. A suitable READ and FORMAT statement would be:

```
        READ(2,10)((MARK(I,J),J=1,4),I=1,3)
     10 FORMAT (8I10)
```

The fact that the READ statement requires twelve integer values to be satisfied does not matter. The FORMAT statement, having exhausted the eight integer specifications on one data card, cycles back on itself and automatically uses the same format specifications for a second data card. On the second data card there are only four values, but again it does not matter. This time, the READ statement is satisfied after reading the fourth value from this card. Reading is automatically terminated, and no further values are sought from the second data card.

In conclusion, where there are large amounts of data to be read from many data cards, and where the format of the data on each of these cards is identical, only the format specifications of the first data card need be stated in the FORMAT statement.

A similar state of affairs exists for WRITE statements. Consider the WRITE and FORMAT statements below:

```
        WRITE (3,10)((MARK(I,J),J=1,4),I=1,3)
     10 FORMAT (11X,4I10,/)
```

The FORMAT statement specifies: 10 blank spaces, then print four integer values and then skip a line of print. But the WRITE statement specifies that 12 integer values are to be printed. The FORMAT statement allows the printing of four values, leaving the required blanks, skips a line of print, allows another four values to be printed, leaving the required blanks again, and so on until all twelve values have been printed. A blank line is left between each of the three sets of four values. Thus, if array MARK contained the values on the data card read in as specified by the READ statement, then the printer output as prescribed by the WRITE and FORMAT statements above would be:

Example 1

Let us examine a program to read in a 6 by 6 array called ARRAY and sum all six columns of the array, storing the answers in a separate one-dimensional array called SUM. Basically, this program is an exercise in inputting and outputting larger arrays than we have used before. The extra summing included in the program adds more interest to the problem. It requires the handling of both one- and two-dimensional arrays in the same program.

113

Flowchart for program:

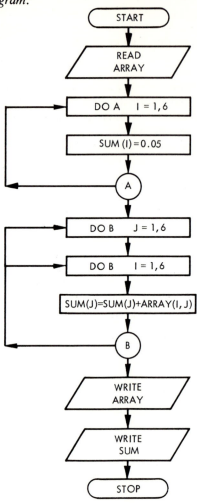

Coding for program:

```
// JOB
// FOR
*LIST SOURCE PROGRAM
*IOCS(CARD, 1132 PRINTER)
C     PROGRAM TO DEMONSTRATE THE HANDLING OF
C     SINGLE AND DOUBLE DIMENSION ARRAYS WITHIN
C     THE SAME PROGRAM
      DIMENSION ARRAY (6,6), SUM(6)
      READ (2,10)((ARRAY(I,J), J = 1,6), I = 1,6)
   10 FORMAT (6F10.1)
```

```
          DO 40 I = 1,6
          SUM (I) = 0.05
       40 CONTINUE
          DO 60 J = 1,6
          DO 60 I = 1,6
          SUM (J) = SUM (J) + ARRAY (I,J)
       60 CONTINUE
          WRITE (3,20)((ARRAY (I,J), J = 1,6), I = 1,6)
       20 FORMAT (20X, 6F8.1,/)
          WRITE (3,20) (SUM(I), I = 1,6)
          CALL EXIT
          END
  // XEQ
          1.1    2.1    3.1    4.1    5.1    6.1
          1.2    2.2    3.2    4.2    5.2    6.2
          1.3    2.3    3.3    4.3    5.3    6.3
          1.4    2.4    3.4    4.4    5.4    6.4
          1.5    2.5    3.5    4.5    5.5    6.5
          1.6    2.6    3.6    4.6    5.6    6.6
```

Printer output:

```
     1.1    2.1    3.1    4.1    5.1    6.1
     1.2    2.2    3.2    4.2    5.2    6.2
     1.3    2.3    3.3    4.3    5.3    6.3
     1.4    2.4    3.4    4.4    5.4    6.4
     1.5    2.5    3.5    4.5    5.5    6.5
     1.6    2.6    3.6    4.6    5.6    6.6
     8.1   14.1   20.1   26.1   32.1   38.1
```

Note

(1) The input format, although describing only one data card, will be
recycled six times. All the 36 values required by the READ statement
are supplied on six data cards, each punched with the same format
and containing six values.

(2) The first DO-loop has been inserted to ensure that all the elements of
array SUM are set to 0·05. This will round all totals accumulated in
SUM to the first decimal place.

(3) The J subscript cycles once for every six cycles of the I subscript.
This means that we are summing all six rows of each column and
putting the answer into SUM(J), which puts the sum total into the
correct column accumulator, i.e. column (J). If SUM(I) had been
used, we would have had at the final sum the row summations
instead of the column summations.

The problem can be extended to sum not only the columns, but also the rows. A realistic application of this is adding columns of marks for different examinations. Each column addition would be the marks of a class of pupils for different examinations, and each row addition would be a single pupil's total for all examinations. This is left as an exercise for the reader and is included in Assignment 10 at the end of this Practical Session. The problem is further extended in the Assignment to work out the average of each column (representing the examination average of each subject) and finally to find the average of all the row summations (representing the pupil's average mark over all the examinations he sat).

If the previous worked example had been one dealing with examination marks, then we would naturally require the pupil's name to be printed alongside his particular row of marks. Up to this point in your programming experience, the only way of doing this would be to devise a program which used a different FORMAT statement for each pupil and to enclose his name in quotation marks so that it would be printed in the output. This would be a most cumbersome program, especially for large numbers of pupils. Moreover, it would not be a general one for use with a different set of pupils, because it would mean that virtually all the FORMAT statements would have to be re-written with the new names. Fortunately, there is an alternative method of coping with this kind of situation.

'A' Format

There are some types of data that are never used in arithmetic operations, for instance, addresses, telephone numbers and names. Some of these data involve numbers, some alphabetic letters, and some both letters and numbers. This kind of data is called *alphanumeric* data. A means of storing this type of data (not used for arithmetic purposes) is by using the '*A*' specification in the FORMAT statement. The letters are then stored in a convenient array in much the same way as numbers are.

Consider the trivial example of storing the name 'John'. Let us decide to store it in an array called NAME. Thus, to read the data card below:

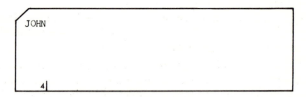

we would write: DIMENSION NAME (4)
　　　　　　　　READ (2,10) (NAME(I), I=1,4)
　　　　　　10 FORMAT (4A1)

Notice the $A1$. This means that we wish to store one alphanumeric character in each array element of NAME. Since there are four characters to be stored, we require $4A1$. After storing, the array elements of NAME would contain the characters shown below:

NAME (1)	NAME (2)	NAME (3)	NAME (4)
J	*O*	*H*	*N*

On the IBM 1130 it is also possible to store two alphanumeric characters per element, in which case $2A2$ would be specified.

Using $A2$: after storing, NAME would contain:

NAME (1)	NAME (2)
JO	*HN*

Thus, we need only use a DIMENSION of NAME (2), instead of NAME (4) as with an $A1$ specification. This saves valuable core space.

Now let us look at the various choices we have of storing information such as a name, using the data card shown below.

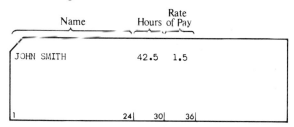

Notice that although the name above requires storage for only ten alphabetic characters, the field reserved for names can contain up to twenty-four characters.

Two alternative methods are available for storing this information:

(a)
```
    DIMENSION NAME (24)
    READ (2,10) (NAME(I),I=1,24), HOURS, RATE
 10 FORMAT (24A1,2F6.1)
```
(b)
```
    DIMENSION NAME (12)
    READ (2,10) (NAME(I),I=1,12), HOURS, RATE
 10 FORMAT (12A2, 2F6.1)
```

It is important to note that whether we use $24A1$ or $12A2$, twenty-four card columns are specified.

To print on the printer output the information read in, we need only list the array in the usual way in a WRITE statement. Obviously, if the alphabetic information has been stored in $A1$ format, then it must be printed out in $A1$ format. The same applies to data stored in $A2$ format.

Example 2

This problem is concerned with processing telephone accounts. It is required to read a deck of data cards, each of which contains customer name, telephone number, and amount owing, and to produce a printed output containing only those customers who owe more than £50. The sum total of all the amounts listed is also to be included in the output.

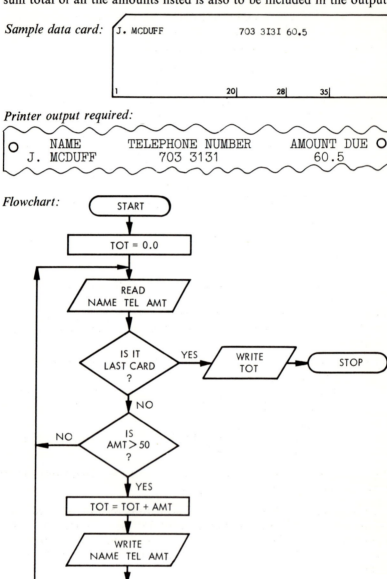

Sample data card:

```
J. MCDUFF              703 3131 60.5


1                      20|      28|     35|
```

Printer output required:

NAME	TELEPHONE NUMBER	AMOUNT DUE
J. MCDUFF	703 3131	60.5

Flowchart:

START

TOT = 0.0

READ NAME TEL AMT

IS IT LAST CARD ? — YES → WRITE TOT → STOP

NO

IS AMT > 50 ? — NO

YES

TOT = TOT + AMT

WRITE NAME TEL AMT

Coding for program:

```
// JOB .T
// FOR
*LIST SOURCE PROGRAM
*IOCS(CARD, 1132 PRINTER)
C     PROGRAM WHICH DEMONSTRATES THE HANDLING
C     OF ALPHANUMERIC DATA
      DIMENSION NAME(10), TEL(8)
      TOT = 0.0
      WRITE (3,5)
    5 FORMAT (28X, 'NAME', 15X, 'TELEPHONE NUMBER',
                           7X, 'AMOUNT DUE')
   50 READ (2,10) (NAME(I), I=1,10), (TEL(I),
                           I=1,8), AMT
   10 FORMAT (10A2, 8A1, F8.1)
      IF (99999.0 - AMT) 20, 30, 20
   20 IF (50 - AMT) 40, 50, 50
   40 TOT _ TOT + AMT
      WRITE (3,60) (NAME(I), I=1,10), (TEL(I),
                           I=1,8), AMT
   60 FORMAT (26X, 10A2, 5X, 8A1, 10X, F8.1)
      GO TO 50
   30 WRITE (3,70) TOT
   70 FORMAT (58X, 'TOTAL AMOUNT', F7.1)
      CALL EXIT
      END
// XEQ
J. SMITH      111 6111      60.5
S. SAMUEL     266 2314     185.9
A. BELL       614 9999      30.5
J. CADBURY    919 7123       6.0
A JONES       666 5164      51.2
                          99999.0
```

Printer output:

	NAME	TELEPHONE NUMBER	AMOUNT DUE
J.	SMITH	111 6111	60.5
S.	SAMUEL	266 2314	185.9
A.	JONES	666 5164	51.2
		TOTAL AMOUNT	297.6

Note

(1) Two different arrays, one for name and the other for telephone number, were chosen. Each one used a different method of storing the alphanumeric information. A single array would have done for both items of information.

(2) The DIMENSION specifications agree with the method of storing.

(3) The last card technique was used to terminate the program.

Example 3

Finally, let us examine the kind of program that could be used in an up and coming application of computers—dating. One of the ways in which a program for computer dating differs from the previous one we examined is that it stores all the names and information to be used. The previous one stored only the data for one person at a time and then went on to process the next person's data.

Suppose we have ten people, each with six recorded characteristics: male/female (1 if male, 0 if female), age, height, weight, sports interests (1 if 'Yes', 0 if 'No'), travel interests (1 if 'Yes', 0 if 'No').

```
MR BROWN A.        1.   26.0 5.5 120.5 1.   0.



1              20|21  25|26  30|31  35|36  40|41  45|46  50|
```

The data for all 10 people could be stored in the form of two-dimensional arrays, e.g.

MR BROWN A.	1.	26.0	5.5	120.5	1.	0.
MISS WHITE J.	0.	29.0	5.3	100.5	0.	1.
—	—	—	—	—	—	—
—	—	—	—	—	—	—
MISS SHAW A.	0.	31.0	5.9	140.0	1.	0.

To find a partner for, say, a MR BLOGGS G, all that need be done is to read into the computer a data card containing the name MR BLOGGS G, together with the set of characteristics he requires in a partner, e.g.

```
MR BLOGGS G.       0.   29.0 5.3 100.5 0.   1.



1              20|21  25|26  30|31  35|36  40|41  45|46  50|
```

This data card is read into the computer and compared with the stored data in the array mentioned above. If a comparison is found, in this case, MISS WHITE J, then the printer output should produce the following:

```
O      MR BLOGGS G. SHOULD MEET MISS WHITE J.      O
```

Flowchart for program:

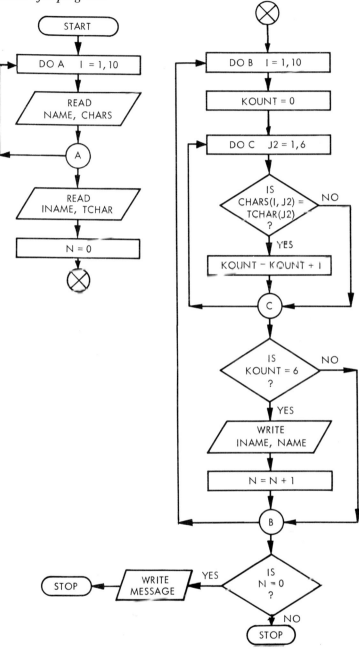

Coding for program:

```
// JOB T
// FOR
*LIST SOURCE PROGRAM
*IOCS(CARD, 1132 PRINTER)
C     COMPUTER DATING PROGRAM
      DIMENSION NAME(10,10), INAME(10),
      DIMENSION CHARS(10,6), TCHAR(6)
      DO 100 I = 1,10
      READ (2,10) (NAME(I,J), J = 1,10),
                            (CHARS(I,J), J = 1,6)
   10 FORMAT (10A2, 6F5.1)
  100 CONTINUE
      READ (2,20) (INAME(I), I = 1,10),
                            (TCHAR(I), I = 1,6)
   20 FORMAT (10A2, 6F5.1)
      N = 0
      DO 200 I = 1,10
      KOUNT = 0
      DO 300 J2 = 1,6
      IF (CHARS (I,J2) - TCHAR(J2)) 200,21,200
   21 KOUNT = KOUNT + 1
  300 CONTINUE
      IF (6 - KOUNT) 200, 22, 200
   22 WRITE (3,30) (INAME(J), J = 1,10),
                          (NAME(I,J), J = 1,10)
   30 FORMAT (10X, 10A2, 'SHOULD MEET', 5X, 10A2)
      N = N + 1
  200 CONTINUE
      IF (N) 24,23,24
   23 WRITE (3,40)
   40 FORMAT (10X, 'NOBODY SUITABLE FOUND')
   24 CALL EXIT
      END
// XEQ
```

```
MR BROWN A.        1.   26.0  5.5   120.5  1.  0.
MISS WHITE J.      0.   29.0  5.3   100.5  0.  1.
MR BIGGS L.        1.   31.5  6.1   145.2  1.  1.
MR WILEY S.        1.   35.2  6.0   150.0  1.  0.
MISS JENNINGS A.   0.   32.0  5.6   102.0  0.  0.
MR ANDREWS J.      1.   25.5  5.9   125.5  1.  1.
MISS WATERS F.     0.   26.2  5.8   110.0  1.  1.
MISS HUNTER C.     0.   29.1  5.8   115.5  1.  0.
MR ROSS F.         1.   36.0  5.9   144.4  1.  1.
MISS SHAW A.       0.   31.0  5.9   140.0  1.  0.
MR WIGAN F.        0.   32.0  5.6   102.0  0.  0.
```

Printer output:

```
 _____~~~~~~~~~_____
| O    MR WIGAN F. SHOULD MEET MISS JENNINGS A.    O |
|_____~~~~~~~~~_____~~~~~~~~~_____|
```

Note

(1) Two two-dimensional arrays are used to store the initial data NAME (10,10) and CHARS (10,6).

(2) The name of the person making the request is stored in INAME (10) and the requested characteristics in TCHAR (6).

(3) KOUNT is used to keep track of the number of successful characteristic matches. If KOUNT is equal to 6, then a complete match has been accomplished.

(4) N is used to keep track of the number of people found suitable. If N is zero at the end of the program, the message 'NOBODY SUITABLE FOUND' is printed.

(5) Since A2 format is being used, only ten storage elements are required for name in arrays NAME and INAME. It allows enough storage for a name of up to 20 characters.

Assignment 10

(1) Write a program to read a data card containing your name, and then print it out on the printer.

(2) Modify the above program to read in your address as well, and then print it out.

(3) A more realistic approach to the computer dating program given in Example 3 would be one in which all individuals whose characteristics were close to the required set of characteristics would have their names printed out. Modify the program to print out all those who have four out of the six required characteristics, and supply a data card to test your program.

(4) Write a program which will store a 7 by 7 array of numbers to be read into the computer. Your program should evaluate the column and row averages and print out not only the original matrix, but also the column and row averages in their appropriate place at the foot of each column or at the end of each row.

(5) Use the three data cards shown below to fill a 6 by 4 matrix:

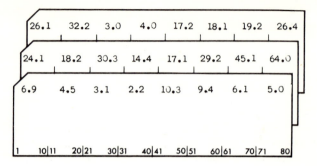

Your program should then proceed to find the largest value in the array.

(6) Modify your program from question (5) so that it will also find the smallest element in the array. Both of these values are to be printed out, together with their matrix subscripts.

Appendix A

H-Code

Text quotes are used with great facility on the IBM 1130, but many machines do not have this capability. Moreover, text quotes are not part of standard Fortran IV. An alternative and widely used method of accomplishing precisely the same objective is to use *H-code*, although it requires careful counting of the number of characters to be printed.

The general form of the H-code specification is:

$$nH$$

where n is the number of characters immediately following the letter H, that are required to be printed.

H is the code used for literal data.

Thus to print out the message:

```
THIS IS LITERAL DATA
```

the FORMAT statement is:

```
FORMAT (20HTHIS IS LITERAL DATA)
```

Note

(1) Any blanks that are to be printed as part of the message must be included as part of the count.

(2) If there is a blank between the H and the first character of the message, then it must be included in the count.

Shown below are two FORMAT statements. The first is the FORMAT statement used in the example program in Practical Session 3 on labelled output. The second is the equivalent FORMAT statement written using H-code:

```
20 FORMAT (20X, 'THE AVERAGE OF', F10.3, ' AND',
                      F10.3, ' IS', F10.3)
20 FORMAT (20X, 14HTHE AVERAGE OF, F10.3, 4H AND,
                      F10.3, 3H IS, F10.3)
```

Thus all example programs shown throughout this book can be converted to run on other computers on which the text quotes facility is not available.

Appendix B

Decimal Points

In Practical Session 2 all the data cards described contained decimal points punched in the various real fields of the data cards. This is not entirely necessary. Consider the following example:

```
       READ (2,10)A,B
10 FORMAT (2F10.2)
```

1	2	3	4	5	6	7	8	9	10	11	12	13	14	15	16	17	18	19	20	21	22	23	24	25	26
						1	6	5	4						5	6	7	8	9						

The above READ statement assigns the values on the data card to the variables *A* and *B* under the control of the FORMAT statement. The FORMAT statement demands that two decimal places are assigned to the incoming values. Thus, the numbers 1654 and 56789 are assigned to *A* and *B* as 16·54 and 567·89 respectively.

If, however, the data card is punched with the decimal points:

1	2	3	4	5	6	7	8	9	10	11	12	13	14	15	16	17	18	19	20	21	22	23	24	25	26
					1	.	6	5	4					0	.	5	6	7	8	9					

the values assigned to *A* and *B* will be 1·654 and 0·56789 respectively, even though the FORMAT requirements demand two decimal places.

The rule is this: if decimal points are punched on the data cards, then the values for assignment are those on the punched card. If no decimal points are punched on the data card, then the values read will be given the number of decimal places laid down by the FORMAT specifications.

This ability to override the decimal portion of the real FORMAT specification, that is, the *d* in the formula *Fw.d*, is a very useful one. It means that, if the data to be used by a previously written program does not conform to the decimal specification of the program, no re-writing of the 'offending' FORMAT statements is required. Note that this argument does not apply to any other part of the above formula.